AF539800

WOMEN ENTREPRENEURSHIP IN SMALL BUSINESS AND MICRO ENTERPRISES

WOMEN ENTREPRENEURSHIP IN SMALL BUSINESS AND MICRO ENTERPRISES

By

Dr. S.Jagadees Pandi

Assistant Professor of Economics
Government Arts College
Karur-5
Tamil Nadu
(India)

DISCOVERY PUBLISHING HOUSE PVT. LTD.
NEW DELHI-110 002

Published by:

Tilak Wasan

DISCOVERY PUBLISHING HOUSE PVT. LTD.

4383/4B, Ansari Road, Darya Ganj
New Delhi-110 002 (India)
Phone : +91-11-23279245, 43596064-65
Fax : +91-11-23253475
E-mail : discoverypublishinghouse@gmail.com
sales@discoverypublishinggroup.com
parul.wasan@gmail.com
web : www.discoverypublishinggroup.com

***First Edition:* 2014**

ISBN: 978-93-5056-439-4

Women Entrepreneurship in
Small Business and Micro Enterprises

Printed at:
Dynamic Printers
Delhi

Preface

Micro enterprises represent an opportunities for women to gain direct access to income when they may have limited avenues for alternative employment. From the economic empowerment point of view, micro-enterprises provide scope for developing and exercising competence in managing an activity, handling funds, taking responsibility for business transaction and taking decisions. Researchers suggest that women-owned micro enterprises are most successful when they are based on non-traditional activities. At the same time the process of starting and operating a new enterprise can be tremendously difficult and involves considerable risk, especially in traditional sector.The Present research intended to provide a deep insight in to the entrepreneurial challenges among the women in traditional as well as micro enterprises in India. I am Pleased to thank the authorities of University Grants Commission (UGC) for having provided me the financial assistance to carry out the study.

I am greatly indebted to the Board of Management of Sree Saraswathi Thyagaraja College, Pollachi, for providing me the infrastructural facilities and an opportunity to do the project.

I am happy to extend my profound thanks to Dr. V. Kulandaiswamy, Principal, Sree Saraswathi Thyagaraja College, Pollachi, for his inspiring Guidance and the interest he evinced in my research work in allocating his precious time for my project discussions.

I wish to express my sincere thanks to Mr. P.Mallaiyarajlu M.A., M.Phil., Project Fellow, for his deep involvement to finish the study.

I Place on record my deepest appreciation to all my family members whose affectionate interest and continued support to all through my research activities.

S. Jagadees Pandi

Contents

List of Abbreviations

BPL	–	Below Poverty Line
GoI	–	Government of India
ILO	–	International Labour Organisation
NABARD	–	National Bank for Agriculture and Rural Development
NBFC	–	Non-Banking Financial Companies
NGO	–	Non-Governmental Organisation
NSSBF	–	National Survey of Small Business Finance
SGSY	–	Swarnjayanti Gram Swarozhar Yojana
SHG	–	Self Help Group

1

Introduction and Design of the Study

The factors determining economic development of any country are natural resources, capital, labour and entrepreneurship. Everywhere in the world, entrepreneurship is seen as one of the most important solutions to unemployment, poverty and low economic growth. The creation of new ventures and growth of existing businesses are vital contributing factors to any economy (Botha et.al 2006). Entrepreneurs are considered to be the most important economic agents for the economic augmentation of a nation.

Entrepreneurship is the process of creating something of value by devoting necessary skills, time and effort, and assuming the accompanying financial and sometimes physical and social risks, to reap the resulting monetary rewards and personal satisfaction. Today entrepreneurship encompasses the ability to organize the various necessary functions of a business and to perceive, appraise and take advantage of opportunities. Factors related to individual and social environment have a direct bearing on the entrepreneurial process, its motivation, innovation, continuity and expansion. (Hisrich and Peter, 1989)

Since the early nineteenth century, economists as well as scholars from other social science disciplines have tried to define the concept in different perspectives. According to

Knight (1921) entrepreneurs are those who take non-quantifiable risks, and profits are rewards that the owner-manager receives for bearing the risks. Weber (1930) discusses entrepreneurship as an expression of cultural values. His emphasis on the importance of cultural factors in the economic development is widely accepted. Schumpeter (1934) sees entrepreneurs as the driving economic force behind a capitalist economy and emphasized the entrepreneur's innovative nature and experimentations with new combinations. Mccleland (1961) explains entrepreneurship as the manifestation of a high need for achievement. Hagen (1962) explains entrepreneurship as a means to obtain recognition. It is a compensation for social marginality. Barth (1967) relates that entrepreneurs are social agents for change.

WOMEN ENTREPRENEURSHIP

The role of women in entrepreneurship is changing rapidly in many countries. The number of women earning income outside the home has been increasing. In addition to their domestic responsibilities for family welfare, childcare, care of the elderly, food preparation and other family task, an increasing number of women generate income by way of establishing business and by being employees in any organisation. Traditionally, women had intensively involved themselves in various activities in agricultural sector. For centuries, women, especially in rural area, had been active in agricultural production, in which, they made food for household consumption. Equipped with the knowledge of agriculture they usually became the major player in local food markets and gradually have become self-employed.

The trend has changed in the new century, where women play a vital role to give an impetus to the development of the country. Today women are working in the modern industrialized fields such as engineering, electronic, readymade garments, fabrics, textiles, pharmaceuticals etc. (Kausik 2009, a). Further, the development of the new economy has brought new opportunities and interests, especially in the area of women's entrepreneurial development. Women are playing more active and multi-faceted roles in society, by starting their own businesses and gradually gaining influence through participation in various economic and social activities (Irene Hvass et.al 2009)

Opportunities for new business or employment that will increase income and wealth are crucial to the development of women's economic welfare. However at all levels of development, the accession of women to the labour market is consistently more difficult than that of men. Employment opportunities as daily wages are often difficult because of their family responsibilities lack of skills, social and cultural barriers. In this context, self-employment or the setting up their own enterprise is highly possible for women to get accession to employment and to income generation. (ILO 1998, a)

Entrepreneurship is a more suitable profession for women than regular employment in public and private sectors since they have to fulfill dual roles. The emergence of women on the economic scene as entrepreneur is a significant development in the emancipation of women. It secures them a place in the society, which they have all along deserved. Entrepreneurial movement among women results in their control over assets and liabilities and freedom to take decisions because a woman as an entrepreneur is more powerful than as a mere worker (Singh, 2006). This will result in uplifting the social status of the women significantly. Through entrepreneurial development a women will not only generate income for her family but will create more employment opportunities for women in society resulting in a multiplier effect in the generation of income and employment.

There are several attempts to define the concept of women entrepreneurship. Women entrepreneur is regarded as a person who accepts a challenging role to quench her ambition to become something, such as to be economically independent by making suitable adjustment between both family and social life (Kausik 2009, b). Women entrepreneurship is the process where women take lead and organise a business or industry and provide employment opportunities to other (Asha and Anuradha 2007, a). Women entrepreneurs may be defined as the women or a group of women who initiate, organize and operate a business enterprise. Any woman or group of women who innovates or adopts an economic activity may be called women entrepreneur (Elena Philip, 2007). According to the government of India, a women entrepreneur is defined as an enterprise owned and controlled by women having a minimum financial interest of 51 per cent of the employment generated in the enterprise to women.

There are different factors associated with the motivation for starting the business by women.

1. ***Personal factors***: women are characteristically independent and pursuer of a sense of achievement.
2. ***Encountering defeat in the previous***: motivation is generated by frustration or discomfort with a previous job, such as being laid-off, employment discrimination and job displacement.
3. ***Improving life***: this motivation comes from suffering a great misfortune. A woman starts a business to maintain the social and economic status of hers and her family.
4. ***Encountering an opportunity:*** some women start their business because they find or encounter opportunities in the market.
5 ***Personal interest;*** some women start their business for the purpose of activating their personal interest into their work, or to put to use what they have learned: women having this type of motivation are mostly housewives with out work experience. Starting a business proves that she is useful and productive to the society.
6. Being capable to take care of the work and the family.
7. To gain freedom and flexibility of selecting her work.

On the other hand, many obstacles to entrepreneurial success have been particularly associated with women's ventures (Berger 1989). Indeed women entrepreneurship is more vulnerable than that of men and this weakness is

reflected in their highest rate of failure (Sherri Grasmuck and Rosario Espinal, 2000). Women entrepreneurs have to face more problems than men entrepreneurs. In most of the cases, women do not have access to productive resources. Their risk taking ability is less. They have to devote time to the family and maintain a balance between their family responsibility and business (Shiva Malik and Rao 2008). Starting and operating business by the women involves considerable risk and effort particularly highest failure rate. Perhaps the rate is higher, if they have to face not only the usual business problems but also their family problems. (Rajani 2008). Another social- cultural constraint specific to women is their expected family role. It addition, the workplace and the duration of the work affect the success rate.

WOMEN ENTREPRENEURSHIP IN INDIA

Women Entrepreneurs have been making a significant impact in the segments of the economy of Eastern countries like USA, Canada, Germany, France, Holland, UK, Sweden etc. and the percentage of women owned small business in the United states is 25 per cent, in Canada 33 1/3 per cent and in France 20 per cent. In the third world countries like East Nigeria 50 per cent of business is done by women and in Ghana 80 per cent are women out of the total business class (Deepa Sharma, 2007).

In India, women constitute about 48 per cent of the population but their participation in economic activity is only 34 per cent. As per 1981 census, women constitute 49.7 per cent of the total population. The women work- force constitutes only 28 per cent of the female population. Out of the total number of self-employed persons, women account for only 5.2 per cent. In 1995 figures of industrial entrepreneurship reveal the participation of women entrepreneurship to 2,95,680 which contribute to a nominal part of the total entrepreneur approximately 2.64 crores in numbers in the country (Urmilaverma and Nidhi, 2007).

According to the 1991 census of India only 4.5 per cent of women are self employed in the country (1,85,900 women).

The figure has risen to 11.2 per cent in 2001 census. Majority of women are engaged in the unorganized sectors like agriculture, agro-based industries, handicrafts, handlooms and cottage based industries. Women participation in the unorganized sectors like agriculture is 64 per cent and the rest is in non-agricultural sectors like construction, mining, quarrying, livestock, plantation, storage, communication etc. But their participation in organized sectors is very low. The proportion in the total employment has remained particularly 1 at 11 per cent. This percentage is less compared to other developing countries (Nalini Shija, 2006)

Table 1.1

Work Participation Rate in India

Fig. in Percentage

Census Year	Category	Persons	Males	Females
1981	Total	36.7	52.6	19.7
	Rural	38.8	53.8	23.1
	Urban	30.0	49.1	8.3
1991	Total	37.7	51.6	22.7
	Rural	40.2	52.5	27.2
	Urban	30.4	49.0	9.7
2001	Total	39.2	51.9	25.7
	Rural	42.0	52.4	31.0
	Urban	32.2	50.9	11.6

Sources: Census Reports of India. Census Reports of India. Census Reports of India.

There is overwhelming evidence that labour force participation of women especially in paid employment, raises the quality of life not only at the household level but also for society at large. The participation of women in economic generation activity not only increases their family income but also brings economic independence among women in the household. Nearly half of the Indian population comprises of women folk but their participation in the economic development of the nation is lower as compared to men, this

is because of the fact that women in India are restricted by the age old cultural and religious dogmas which prevent them from taking an active part in economic activities.

The Census of India calculates the employment status of women on the basis of work participation rate. The Census defines work as a participation in economically productive activity with or without compensation, wages or profit (GoI 2001). Work participation rate of women in India is 19.7 per cent in 1981 Census and increased to 25.7 per cent in 2001 Census. It further showed that work participation among urban female is comparatively lower than of rural women, and much lower than the male work participation rate in both urban and rural areas.

MICRO ENTERPRISES AND WOMEN ENTREPRENEURSHIP

Micro enterprises can play a dominant role in developing countries like India. The development of these enterprises at the grass root level is a powerful medium to ameliorate several social-economic problems such as reduction of poverty, balanced regional development of goods and services appropriate to the local needs, redistribution of both income and opportunities in the community in general. The redistribution of wealth and opportunities lead to decentralization of economic power in the underdeveloped economy (Bhagyavathi, 2008). Potentially it offers unlimited opportunities to produce goods and services, using local resources and generating self-employment opportunities. (Chitsike, 2000)

Small Business is normally a single owner operated business, started with (or) without any employee and with as little capital as possible. It also takes the name of micro-enterprise in the modern business terminology, which means, a term that refers to the countless tiny business begun by the poor in the cities, towns, and villages, known by economists as the "informal economic sector" (Rao 2007). The size of small business or micro enterprises may be defined according to various criteria including the number of workers, the volume of output (or) sales, the value of assets, the use of energy etc., The criteria of the number of workers is the most widely used, because of its apparent simplicity and data on the other criteria are generally lacking. (ILO 1998, b)

Micro-Enterprises are defined as firms employing between one to ten workers and they encompass self-employed side walk merchants with only a few dollars worth of stock, as well as shop owners and traders with thousands of dollars investment. (Xavier et.al 2008).

The definition of micro-enterprise varies from country to country. In the United States for example, micro-enterprises are those with employees and less, while a small business is categorized as one with more than 5 to 500 employees. In New Zealand, 99.5 per cent of small business have less than 100 employees and account for 60.3 per cent of employment. Of these small business, the majority are micro-enterprises. In Peru, small firms are defined as businesses with up to 20 employees and an average per capital investment not exceeding US $ 10,000 and a maximum investment of US $ 20,000 (Anna de Bruin, 1999).

There are mixed responses about the development of micro enterprises. To some observers, this is an encouraging sign, that markets are functioning and people are finding opportunities to participate in ways that empower and nourish many, particularly those who are otherwise most disadvantaged. These enterprises are usually started with low capital investment, but contribute significantly to the development and growth of rural economy. It promotes potential for creating self-employment avenues for unemployed rural population. Unlike large scale industries tiny enterprises do have insignificant pollution effect on environment.

To other observers, however, this increase in the number of people engaged in micro and small enterprises is a sign of failure of the economy to provide productive jobs that people are forced to take refuge in activities that provide only minimal and subsistence poverty. More over these enterprises adopt limited marketing policies and a high percentage of idle capacity such as the majority of business firms have no brand names for their products and sell from their location with no special distributor (Carl Liedholm, 2001). Further it is more difficult for these enterprises to deliver production of a consistent quality that meet the required production standards.

Though the above argument is not in favour of the development of micro-enterprises, researches establish the fact that it is a potential escape route for unemployed and low income people, and it becomes the engine of growth in developing countries. Worldwide micro enterprises coupled with micro credit is considered as one of the most effective measure to overcome poverty and improve the living standards of rural agricultural population. (Jariah et.al 2003)

WOMEN IN MICRO-ENTERPRISE AND SMALL BUSINESS

Micro enterprises represent an opportunities for women to gain direct access to income when they may have limited avenues for alternative employment. From the economic empowerment point of view, micro-enterprises provide scope for developing and exercising competence in managing an activity, handling funds, taking responsibility for business transaction and taking decisions (Asha and AnuRadha 2007, b). Researches suggest that women-owned micro enterprises are most successful when they are based on non-traditional activities.

However, many researchers observed that women involvement in micro-enterprises are largely concerned with survival of their family and themselves rather than running a successful business. Women, earning low income in rural and urban areas by engaging themselves as home-based workers (Producers) petty traders and hawkers, producers and supplier of services could he defined as micro-enterprises. They are mostly illiterates, arising from lower strata of society (in terms of caste and community) with low level of skills, mostly involved in their households work and with no work experience. They enter into micro-enterprise sector out of economic compulsions, to supplement family income and incase of women headed households, to earn livelihood for the family (Perera 1995). Because of their background they have little chance to get wage employment in organized sector, most of them operate from their own homes, use low technology and cater to the local and lower end of the market segment; and micro-enterprises are mostly their part time occupation, characterized by irregular house work. These business are almost funded from family savings and small loans from informal money lenders. Inadequate investment capital coupled with low levels of skills compels them to adopt low technology based production process and the inadequacy of working capital forces the women to buy raw material in small quantities making it costlier. All this affects their cost of production adversely. This also limits their ability to experiment or to introduce new products (or) designs (Howrath, 1992).

Though the above studies expressed a negative imagination of women in micro enterprise sector, it is represented as a potential route for attaining the empowerment of women, whose are disadvantaged in the society. The rationale for supporting the development of women-headed micro and small enterprises is two folded. Firstly it contributes to poverty alleviation. Secondly it promotes women's economic and social empowerment (ILO 1998, c). Participation of a women in enterprise sector leads to:

1. An increase in the control over and or ownership of resource within the household economic portfolio.
2. Leads to increased self-esteem and self confidence and in turn increased mobility and interaction at the household and community levels.
3. Leads to well defined economic vision for the future. More generally, it is a recognized matter that the main vehicles for economic growth are the micro and small enterprise. Therefore, as a matter of economic efficiency, it is important to ensure that potential women entrepreneur is not left out of any development process.

4. These businesses are especially significant to the household women since they rely on fewer alternative sources of income and devote proportionally more of their income to the welfare of their household than men do.

DESIGN OF THE STUDY

Statement of the Problem

Women in micro enterprises and small business open a new area, women entrepreneurship for investigation in the socio-economic environment in India. The perspective of women, particularly in rural area, is gradually changing with the growing sensitivity of the roles, responsibilities and social and economic status of the women in the society in general and family in particular due to their involvement in micro enterprises sector. At the same time the process of starting and operating a new enterprise is tremendously difficult and involves considerable risk, especially in traditional sector, because she often lacks the management skills, education, adequate family and societal support system to facilitate her efforts.

Reviews of literature have made it evident that few studies have been conducted on women entrepreneurship in micro enterprises, studying different entrepreneurial aspects at different geographical areas. The nature of problem experienced by women entrepreneurs in micro enterprise sector in Coimbatore District in Tamilnadu was thought to be an area yet less explored and motivated to conceptualize the present research. It would be quite pertinent that a research study is carried out in this district to examine the issues faced by the women entrepreneurs in small business and especially micro entrepreneurs, who belong to Self Help Groups (SHG) in Tamilnadu. The study looks at the various issues of women such as work life imbalance, marketing, finance and future aspirations etc...

Concepts and Variables

The following concepts and variables are used in the study.

- *Mahalir Thittam* is a socio-economic empowerment programme for women implemented by Tamil Nadu Corporation for Development of Women Ltd. Mahalir Thittam is based on Self Help Group (SHG) approach and is implemented in partnership with Non Governmental Organisations (NGOs) and Community based organisations
- *Entrepreneurial intensity:* it is the measure of level of commitment to the entrepreneurial endeavour. It can be characterized as the passion required for entrepreneurial success.
- *Work life balance*: it is about being able to maintain a balance between work and personal responsibilities on such as work and family, work and personal fulfillment, work and community responsibility.
- The demographic variables in the study include age, community, religion, educational qualification, previous occupation.
- Details of enterprises include nature and type of enterprise, capital investment, and financial assistance.
- Motivational factors which include risk taking and achievement of motivation.
- Issues related to work life imbalance; business profit and growth demand time and household activity, child care and personal interest etc. which can create inter-personal and intra personal conflicts.
- Economic issues of enterprise which arise before and during the enterprise, like obtaining bank loan, marketing etc.
- Level of Satisfaction of women entrepreneur, the strategies and plan for further expansion and success of the enterprise.

Objectives

The major objectives of the study are:

1. To review the profile of women entrepreneurs in small business and micro enterprises.

2. To explore the problems of women entrepreneurs in balancing household chores and business responsibilities.
3. To identify the various economic issues unique to women in setting up and running the business and enterprises.
4. To give remedial measures for the effective performance of the women entrepreneurs in small business and micro enterprises.

Methodology

The Universe of the Study

The women entrepreneurs who belong to Self Help Groups (SHG) in the Taluks of Palladam, Pollachi and Udumalpet Taluk of Coimbatore District, Tamil Nadu.

Sampling Frame

Multi Stage sampling technique has been adopted. Coimbatore is one among the districts having the highest number of SHGs in Tamilnadu, which is the reason for choosing the district. In the first stage 3 Taluks were taken for the study. In the second stage 75 SHGs were identified, each Taluk covering 25 SHGs. In the third stage 450 SHG members, holding different categories of small business and micro enterprises, have been randomly chosen as the sample for the study.

Sources of Data

The present study is empirical in nature and has been studied mainly by primary data. A structured questionnaire has been used to collect the necessary data from the women entrepreneurs selected for the study. The secondary data have been used to a limited extent as the selected topic is explanatory in nature. The supported data were collected from the collector's office, official records of SHGs etc,. In addition to this, focal group discussions were conducted among the heads of SHG members to supplement the data and information.

Tools of Analysis

The results of study have been presented with suitable statistics such as Percentages and Factor Analysis and Reliability analysis.

Research Questions

To meet the objectives of the study attempts are made to shed light on the following questions.

1. What is the major motivation for business?
2. What is the reason to choose traditional business?
3. Do women entrepreneurs balance the house hold work and business work?
4. What were the major economic problems in the area of finance, marketing and running the business?
5. What were the strategies adopted by them to continue the business (or) expanding the business?

On the basis of these research questions a research study has been conducted.

Scope of the Study

The present research intends to provide a deep insight into the entrepreneurial challenges faced by among the women in traditional as well as micro enterprises in India. This study seeks to determine diverse set of factors that facilitate and obstruct the growth of women entrepreneurs in small business and micro enterprises. It identified and addressed key challenges faced by the women entrepreneurs under the support of Self help group. The problems faced by the respondents would serve as an informative experience guiding the existing and the new emerging women entrepreneurs. It would also assist the policy makers at government and non-government level to understand the problems of women entrepreneurs more precisely and pragmatically and thus modify and plan their programmes based on the actual desire needs.

Limitations

1. The findings are not unique to women entrepreneurship because the study has no comparative data on the male entrepreneur in micro enterprise sector.
2. All respondents are from one sector named self help group and so the results may (or) may not be applicable to the other micro enterprise sectors run by women.

3. The study looks only at women in small business and micro enterprises. No conclusion about women entrepreneurs in general can be arrived at.

REFERENCES

1. Anna de Bruin (1999) "Women *and Entrepreneurship—Rationale for Micro Enterprise Development*", Paper Presented at the APEC Study Centre Consortium Conference, Auckland, May 31-June 2.
2. Asha Patil and Anuradha Mathu (2007) "Women *and Entrepreneurship—Issues and Challenges,* Kalpaz Publications, Delhi.
3. Barth. F (1967) "On the Study of Social Change" *American Anthropologist,* Vol. 68, December, pp. 661-669.
4. Bhagyavathi, venugopal, Nagesha G & Nagabhusanam K (2008) "Participation Level of Farm Women in Entrepreneurship Activities under Self-Help Groups", *Mysore Journal of Agricultural Science,* Vol. 42, No. 1, pp. 159-162.
5. Berger M, and Byvinie. M (1989) "*Women Ventures*" West Hartford CT, Kumarian Press.
6. Botha.M, Nieman G.H and Van Vuumen (2006) "Evaluating the Women Entrepreneurship Training Programme: A South African Study" *The International Indigenous Journal of Entrepreneurship,* Vol. 2, No. 1, October.
7. Carl Liedholm (2002) "Small Firm Dynamics: Evidence from Africa and Latin America", *Small Business Economics,* Vol. 18, No. 1/3, Special Issue: Small Firm Dynamism in East Asia, pp. 227-242.
8. Chitsike Colletah (2000) "Cultural as a Barrier to Rural Women's Entrepreneurship; Experience from Zimbabwe", *Gender and Development,* Vol. 8, No. 1, pp. 71-77.
9. Deepa Sharma (2007) " Women Entrepreneurship–Problems, Solutions and Future Prospects of Development, "(ed) Sanjay Diwari & Anusha Diwari" "*Women Entrepreneurship and Economic Development*", Sarup & Sons Publishers, New Delhi.
10. Elena Philip (2007) "Women Entrepreneurship—Challenges and Prospects"(ed) Sanjay Diwari & Anusha Diwari" *Women Entrepreneurship and Economic Development*" Sarup & Sons Publishers, New Delhi.

11. Government of India, *Census India Report 2001*, Office of the Register General and Census Commissioner, New Delhi.
12. Hagen E.E (1962) "*On the Theory of Social Change: How Economic Growth Begins*, Homewood, Illinois: Dorsey.
13. Hisrich R.D , Peter M.P. (1989) "*Entrepreneurship, Starting, Developing and Managing a New Enterprise*" Richard D.Irvin, Bostan.
14. Howrath. R (1992) "Women's Micro Enterprise – Lessens for Enterprise Support Agencies" (ed) *Development of Micro Enterprises by Women*, British Council Division.
15. International Labour Organisation (1998), "*Gender Issues in Micro-Enterprise Development: A Briefing Note*", The International Small Enterprise Programme (ISEP), June.
16. Jaria M, Laily. P Mumtazha. O, and Aini. S, (2003) "Report on Mechanisation & Technological Adoption: Scaling up Micro Enterprises to Small Scale Enterprise: Serdang: *Monograph Series on Social Science*, Penerbit University, Putra Malasia.
17. Knight. F. (1921) "*Risk, Uncertainty and Profit*" Bostan; Houghton Mifflin.
18. Kausik D.S. (2009) "*Women Entrepreneurship*" Ritu Publications, Jaipur.
19. Mcclelland D.C. (1961) "*The Achieving Society*" Collier-Mcmillain, Toranto.
20. Nalini Shija Chanamban (2006) " *Women Entrepreneurship in North Eastern Region of India-Problems and Prospects*, Vista International Publishing House, Delhi.
21. Perera L.(1998) "Women in Micro and Small Scale Enterprises Development in Srilanka (ed) "*Women in Micro and and Small Enterprise Development*" Dignard. L and Hvet. J Boulder: Westview Press.
22. Rajani N (2008) "Management Training Needs Women Entrepreneurs" *Anthropologist*, Vol. 10, No. 4, pp. 277-281.
23. Rao M.B (2007) "A Small Business — An Avenue of Self Employment" online Paper available at www.indianmba.com/Faculty_Column/FC527/fc527.html
24. Schumpeter. J.A.(1934) " *The Theory of Economic Development*" Cambridge Mass; Harverd University Press.
25. Shiva Malik and Taranjit Kaur Rao (2008) "Profile of Women Entrepreneurs—A Case Study of Chandigarh" Political Economy Journal of India, Vol. No. January-June.

26. Sherri Grasmuck and Rosario Espinal (2000), "Market Success or Female Autonomy? Income, Ideology, and Empowerment Among Micro Entrepreneurs in the Dominican Republic", *Gender and Society,* Vol. 14, No. 2, pp. 231-255.
27. Singh B.K.(2006) " *Women Empowerment Through Self-Help Groups*", Adhyayan Publishers, Delhi.
28. Urmilaverma Nidhi Srivastava (2007) "Women Entrepreneurship—Key to Women Empowerment and Self Reliance" "(ed) Sanjay Diwari & Anusha Diwari" *Women Entrepreneurship and Economic Development*" Sarup &sons Publishers, New Delhi.
29. Weber. M. (1930) "The *Protestant Ethic and the Sprit of Capitalism*", Translated by Parsons", Scribner, Newyork.
30. Xavier M.J , Raja J, Usha Nandhini.S, (2008), Impact Assessment of a Rural Women's Micro Entrepreneurship Project Using Path Analysis Models" *IIMB Management Review*, Vol. 20, No. 2, June.

2

Review of Earlier Studies

Having briefly reviewed the entrepreneurship scenario in various perspectives, it would be pertinent to review the literature on women entrepreneurship in micro enterprise sector. There are many studies available, examining the profile of women entrepreneurs and the issues of micro enterprise sectors. Most of the studies dealt with here are based on the empirical analysis from different parts of the world. The literature review is presented for the countries other than India in one section and for India in another section, in a concise and coherent pattern on chronological order.

STUDIES FROM COUNTRIES AROUND THE WORLD OTHER THAN INDIA

Ingoid Verheul[1] et.al., (2009) investigated time allocation decisions in new ventures of female and male entrepreneurs using a model that distinguishes between effects of preferences and the productivity on the number of working hours. The findings of the study showed that individuals have a lower preference for work time if they have other income sources. Such people are more risk averse and are not motivated to start a business by being one's own boss. Productivity of time is positively related to financial capital invested, industry and relevant experience, and the prevalence of outsourcing activities. Being gender conscious, women invest fewer hours in the firm than men. They prefer lower average of work time and a lower productivity per hours worked. This can be explained by the availability of other income and the risk adverse nature of women. The lower female productivity is due to lower levels of human, social and financial capital and the fact is that women run relativity small firms.

Bekele[2] et al (2008) conducted a study in Ethiopia to identify key predictors of long term survival and viability in small businesses and enterprises, of both male and female entrepreneurs. The result indicated that 53 per cent of the 110 businesses that failed during the period of study were businesses that were operated by women who experienced difficulty in securing loans from commercial banks. Female headed firms that ceased operation had an average lifetime of 3.2 years, while male headed firms that ceased operation had on average life time of 3.9 years. The study has shown that in Ethiopia, although women initiate more new businesses in comparison with men, they find it relatively harder to grow their businesses to the next higher level mostly due to lack of access of finance, technical skills and policy related support from Government.

Adereni[3] et.al (2008) had assessed the choice and performance of women in technological and non-technological micro and small scale enterprises in Southwest Nigeria. Firstly the research sheds light on the learning mechanism of the entrepreneur. It included self- conceptualization, friends, business contacts and associations among others. Secondly the study showed unemployment as the major motivation for starting non technological business ownership and personal interest for technological startups. Thirdly many of the entrepreneurs requested for financial assistance from government to enable their business. Fourthly the study investigated some theoretical factors that were responsible for the choice of technological and non venture. The three learning mechanism such as television, trade fair, community outreach programmes were more relevant to choose technological venture.

Muhammad[4] (2008) analysed gender related challenges faced by women entrepreneurs in the context of the socio economic landscape in Pakistan. The significant findings from the study were that almost 70 per cent of the respondents had close male relatives working in business, at the time of the start up of their business. A total of 48 per cent respondents express the need to maintain or improve their personal as well as socio economic status of the family. In many cases, this was triggered by an unhappy event, such as the death or retirement of their husband. More over a significant number of women in the study (31.7%) were no longer content with their role as a homemaker. Most of the respondents within this category were relatively older women with little or no previous experience. Only 20 per cent of the sample made a conscious decision to enter business in order to benefit from the freedom to choose their own kind of work hours, environment etc,

William[5] (2008) investigated micro and small locally export business owners in the manufacturing and agriculture sector in Jamaica. The study highlighted that the owners of these small and micro firms expressed their inability to expand production as a major problem for export expansion. Many of them mentioned the need to have more space to be able to operate at their full potential. They also lamented the lack of highly qualified workers. The more qualified workers go to work for multinationals or larger firms. These factors, they opine, have the impact on their ability to produce to the full potential. Therefore, there is no excess capacity for export. Furthermore, the study indicated that, saturated domestic market is not very influential in inducing export market entry. The Jamaican market by any measure is very small. Analyzing these stimuli, that have the relatively highest influence in export initiation, export of these small and micro firms becomes important for competitive reasons, although the domestic market is saturated.

Francis[6] et.al (2006) conducted a study in Northern Ireland to assess women entrepreneur's perception of the experience of raising finance and subsequent growth and development of their business. The result of the study indicated that the source of finance is a problematic issue. This is despite the fact that the investigation of the supple side revealed no evidence of conscious discrimination against women- owned businesses on the part of the six main banks in Northern Ireland. The finding of phase one revealed that the main banks prefer to find expansions rather than start-ups. Overall the respondents had negative perception of banks as source of finance.

Selvamalar[7] (2006) examined the demographic profile of Tamil women entrepreneurs in the North East of Srilanka who became entrepreneurs as a result of war. Five main areas of interest were examined viz.:

1. characteristics of these women;
2. factors that spurred them into entrepreneurship;
3. Challenges;
4. measure of success used; and
5. demographic profile.

Research finding indicates that a large percentage of these women were highly entrepreneurial having motivation to achieve a higher standard of living by being self-reliant and supportive to their families. Most of these women were married considered business as a means to an end, as many had lost their husbands in the war. A large majority of these women were in business for the first time and retain them business as successful venture. Their measures of success were self-fulfillment and a balance between family and work.

Shellon[8] (2006) analysed the work-family conflict in women entrepreneurship and presented that work and family management strategies will improve venture performance for women-owned businesses. She argued that work family management strategies are significant determinants of venture growth and that role-sharing strategies are preferred by most women because these options permit them to enjoy the enhancement of both work and family roles reducing the level of inter role conflict. Moreover women who build management and workers teams are able to handle family emergencies without disrupting business operations and consequently suffer reduced firm performance. By reducing the level of personal involvement required by the entrepreneur in the business, participative management practices allow increased involvement in the family role.

Morris[9] et.al (2006) analyzed the growth aspiration of women entrepreneurs. The entrepreneurs were separated into two categories for the purpose of analysis. Those who had experienced growth of more and less than1$ million were placed in the high growth and modest growth categories. The study indicated that the high growth entrepreneur seemed less concerned with resources currently in place than with the desire to create and build wealth. These entrepreneurs had a tendency to strongly identify business as an extension of one's self-concept. The moderate growth entrepreneurs on the other hand, used words such as sustainable income and family financial security as motivational factors for starting their businesses. These entrepreneurs preferred to control growth at levels in line with their cost practices life styles and family needs. They tended to view the businesses more as a tool or vehicle for income substitution, financial security and a means of accommodating other life priorities.

Heino[10] (2006) analysed the financial factors related the micro enterprise access to credit markets and identified the relationship between liquidity constraints and the creation of micro enterprises in Mexico. The result of the study indicated that there is a positive relationship between the probabilities of starting a micro enterprise and needing to largely finance it using personal savings implies that liquidity constraints hinder the creation of micro enterprise in Mexico. The results indicate furthermore, that only small numbers of owners starting up a micro enterprise were able to rely on the formal sector institutions to provide them the start up loan. This is because liquidity constraints hinder many individuals from creating a business. This implies that increasing the availability and participation of the formal and informal lenders in the creation of micro enterprises in Mexico is a challenge for policy makers.

Elizabeth[11] et.al (2006) analyzed the management competencies of women business owners in Western Australia. In terms of current skills respondents felt most competent in the areas of customer service skills and people management skills. Similarly they felt least competent in the area of electronic communicative skills, which is similar to their initial competencies. Respondents also reported improvement on all items with few gender differences, other than women still reporting higher customer service skills. Moreover, the study indicated that, even though most respondents rated themselves as competent on all current items they required further training in all items. For most small business owners, training represented a very small proportion of their annual budget, with almost half (49%) of respondents budgeting less than $ 500 per year for training, irrespective of gender. There are clearly contradictory results showing the requirement of training on numerous areas but the absence of a line item for training.

A study (2005) was conducted by Kathleen and Asya[12] among Ten Arab women from Bahrain and Oman on the business start-up experiences. The results of the study indicated that the Bahraini and Oman women chose to engage in service sector businesses. Although the participants were well educated like their western counterparts they have limited real businesses experiences and lack key managerial skills important to run a business. These women did not cite gender discrimination as a problem either in establishing or operating their businesses despite encountering many of the very same obstacles of their female entrepreneurs elsewhere. On the other hand, they find themselves unable to compete in certain markets or partake freely of available resources as a result of the culturally-enforced separation of men from women which not only limits their business owner access but also reduces their opportunity for networking information gathering etc.

Gray[13] (2005) et.al, examined a description of negative stereo type of women entrepreneurs in Morocco. The study revealed that approximately 87 per cent of Moroccan women entrepreneurs would either expand or maintain their operations over half (53.3%) of the entrepreneurs and expressed an inclination to expand. One third (33.3%) desired to hold and maintain while the remaining minority (13.3) noticed a preference to harvest of cash in their investment. The study further explains that the situation for the middle and the upper middle class Moroccan women entrepreneurs appears to be different in many regards. The upper middle class women seem to use their dependence on their spouse in order to create a sort of bank account of independence for further needs. Women of lower economic classes engage in marketing are said to cross the boundaries of private and public as their public defines them. But women of higher economic status are still considered by the boundaries of their culturally defined public and private domains.

Joan Winn[14] (2005) reviewed the barriers associated with women entrepreneurship. She argued that women entrepreneurs are often excluded from trade and business associations and informal net workers. This has a negative impact on their access to information, credit training, business partners and new market entry. The author further explained that, while career opportunities for women have changed, family role models typically have not. Most young women see their mother doing the lion's share of home chores. For married women, especially those with children, business ownership takes its toll in stress and, in many cases, result in divorce. Even with a stable marital relationship to mitigate risk child rearing responsibilities can interfere with the best of intentions. She suggested that while many mothers become successful business owners, the difficulties of balancing their families with their business obligations cannot be over emphasized.

Helen Appas[15] (2004) conducted case studies on mainly women's micro enterprises in rural areas of the USA. The study disclosed that 44 per cent of respondents reported that they are not able to contribute business earnings for household support because their businesses are so new that earnings are re-invested in the business. The American women who do traditional crafts report that their earning is limited because of the part-time nature of their craft work. The remaining 50 per cent who contribute to household economics are able to provide from 25 to 100 per cent of the household income. According to the study most women stated that they are pleased with the success of their business. They want to stay close to family and culture, and they have chosen food service as an option.

Robb[16] (2002) conducted a study to compare how business survival varies between men and women who owned business start-ups and between minority and non minority owned business start-ups. The results indicate that some of the differences were observed in survival rates for new firms. It showed that the black male owned businesses were 51 per cent more likely to close, while black female owned businesses were 38 per cent more likely to close. On Hispanic owned business, the men were 11 per cent more likely to close than white male owned business. While those owned by Hispanic females 23 per cent were more likely to close. Businesses owned by both male and female Asians fared better than businesses owned by white males. Businesses owned by 14 per cent of Asians males were less likely to close, while those owned by 16 per cent Asian females were less likely to close. In the case of both blacks and Asians, businesses owned by females were less likely to close than their male counterparts.

Carlied Holm[17] (2002) investigated the determinants of survival and growth of very small enterprises in Africa and Latin America. The study disclosed that the more likely variable to affect the growth of existing enterprises would be location. Firms located in urban and commercial areas are more likely to survive during a given year than those located in rural areas or those being operated out of home. Urban and commercial location is also associated with faster growth, as measured by the number of employees hired in a given year. The study further explained that, the variables such as sector, location, country and the human capital are important determinants for the expansion of very small enterprises. Controlling for the influence of other variables enterprise growth in most cases is inversely related to initial size and age of the enterprise. In addition, the above variables are shown to significantly influence its ability to add workers.

A study (2001)[18] attempted to identify the strategic paths chosen by women entrepreneurs and the relation of those paths to the growth orientation of the firm. Gundry study showed that the high growth oriented entrepreneurs were clearly different from the low growth-oriented entrepreneurs on several dimensions. The former were much more likely to select strategies for their firms that permitted greater focus on market expansion and new technologies to exhibit greater intensity towards business ownership. These entrepreneurs tended to have a more structured approach to organizing their business. It also suggests a more disciplined perception of managing the firm.

Hatun U fuk[19] (2001) carried out a study in Ankara in Turkey to determine the profile of women entrepreneurs. The three most important factors influencing women in becoming entrepreneurs were meeting the family needs, initiating social relations and fulfilling personal needs. The most important problems that arose during start-up of their business were provision of capital, bureaucratic procedures and lack of experience. The women rated the individual characteristics required in entrepreneurship as self confidence, courage, communication skills, patience and modesty. The finding shows that whether they were employed or not before the patterns of expenditure significantly differed according to their education level at $P< 0.01$. Regarding the period of entrepreneurship, the patterns of spending the income that they acquired through entrepreneurship is found significant at $P< 0.01$, also the work they did before and their plan for the future depending on their entrepreneurship period, was found significant at $P< 0.05$ level.

Muriel Orhan[20] (2001) analyzed the financial discrimination among the business owners in France. The study revealed that the gender of the entrepreneur is part of the decision making process and the female applications is considered as a disadvantage. Furthermore, the entrepreneurs of such business may themselves be reluctant to borrow small amount of money, as the interest rate would be substantially higher than for bigger projects. Many involved in business financing deny the existence of gender bias stating that they are looking for an entrepreneur profile. One possible problem is that many female applicants may not fit the 'stereotype' entrepreneur profile being assertive, competitive self-confident and experienced. Due to some real (or) perceived lack of financial competencies women may have more difficulty in developing a medium term plan. Moreover the French women are reported to feel insecure in financial negotiations.

Holy Buttner[21] (2001) conducted a study to examine whether relational theory could be used to classify women entrepreneur's comments about the ways they managed employees and worked with client in their business. The study explained that sixty nine of these women made at least one comment that was relational in nature about their client, employee relationship. Of the total 312 comments, 155 comments fell into one relational category, 118 comments describe preserving activities, and 86 comments describe empowering activities. The finding from the study suggests that relational theory is a useful frame for examining the ways women entrepreneurs approach relationships in their businesses. The sample entrepreneurs reported that they believed that increasing the competence of their employees would enhance the success of their firms.

Lee and Rendell[22] (2001) analysed the role of self-employment in differentiating the working lifetime of blacks and women from men in the USA. The results of the study indicated the working experience of the black and white women is lesser than white men in self employment. Blacks and White women experience fewer lifetime entries to and shorter duration in self employment than white men. But the White and Black women experience more entries to wage employment than do white men. Women and Blacks experience fewer transitions in both directions between wage employment and self employment. These race and gender difference in the extent of lifetime self-employment and patterns of transition, between employment statuses suggest that underlying patterns of women and the Black's self-employment behaviour contribute more to employment disadvantage over their lifetimes than doe's wage-employment behaviour.

Verheul and Roy[23] (2001) analysed the uses of start-up capital of both male and female entrepreneurs. The study showed that female entrepreneurs have a smaller amount of start-up capital than their male counterparts, but they do not significantly differ with respect to the composition of financial capital. When investigating the impact of gender on the size and composition of start-up capital, a distinction is made between an indirect and direct effect. The indirect effect is represented by the way women differ from men in terms of type of business and management and experience. The difference are female entrepreneurs wish to do part-time, work, wish to work in the service sector, aversion to singleness, less financial management experience. The direct effect can't be attributed to these differences and is called a gender effect. It is interpreted that, the smaller amount of financial capital of female entrepreneurs may be attributed to a lack of confidence in their own entrepreneurial capabilities.

Heshmati[24] (2001) analysed the relationship between the size, and the age growth rate of firms for a large sample of micro and small firms in Sweden. The results indicated that there is a direction of changes in the expected growth rate of variables of interest, due to changes in the age and size of firms; it is not always in accordance with the expected (negative)outcomes. Employment, assets and sale do not necessarily develop the same relationship between the age and the size of firms. These positive relationships might be due to the relatively young age of the firms. The fact is that large and older firms have the advantage of having established finance, goods and services. A positive relationship between growth in sales and size of firms defined in terms of the number of employees indicates that the presence of scale effects improves labour productivity. Moreover, indebtednesses of the firm negatively affects the growth rate of assets (sales) while it has no impact on employment, whilst labour market and human capital variables show little positive impact on the growth of firms.

Anna[25] et.al (2000) compared the differences between traditional and non -traditional women business owners in Illinois of the USA. The analysis revealed that significant differences exist between the two groups on several of the independent variables. It showed that traditional business owners had higher venture efficacy for opportunity recognition, higher career expectations of life balance and security and they reported that financial support received from others was more important to them than those in non-traditional businesses. On the other hand, the non-traditional owners had higher venture efficacy for planning and higher career expectations for money (or) wealth than the traditional group. Moreover venture efficacy and career expectation of autonomy were positively related to sales in traditional and non- traditional business owner while the expectation of money or wealth was negativity related.

Priscilla Chu[26] (2000) described the characteristics of Chinese female entrepreneurs in Hong Kong. According to the study the cause of business start-up was basically culture related. The entrepreneurs view of assisting their husbands and fulfilling the wishes of their parents were the key reasons for the startup. The study also reconfirms that cultural difference is more salient than industrial sector or gender in personality profiles. There are a few dimensions that are rather similar for all entrepreneurs. They tend to see themselves as neither realistic non idealistic, neither relaxed nor anxious and more goal oriented than uncertain. The study also explains that different motivation patterns are mainly due to gender difference; different personality traits results in different patterns of entrepreneurial behaviours.

Grasmuk and Espinal[27] (2000) examined the impact of gender on the relative economic success of micro entrepreneur and their contribution to family income. The study highlighted that, while both male and female entrepreneurs tend to assert equal (or) dominant decision making in all matters or in household expenses increases in relative income contribution augment both groups general decision making. More over income apparently matters at different gender households. In other words, when income does matter, the impact of income kicks it at a much lower level for women than for men. And though this is an income effect, it is simultaneously a culture effect since it is structured by cultural notions of men as dominant breadwinners and women as producers of supplemental, with the income by them.

Greg Hundley[28] (2000) analysed the male-female caring differences in self employment. The study highlighted, among the self- employed, female earnings decreases with marriage, family size, and hours of housework, while male earnings are positively associated with the same variables. The study suggested that women and men who are self employed specialize more intensively in housework and market work than do their organisational employed counterparts, which explains in part why the male/female earning gap is larger for the self employed than for the organisationally employed. Among women marriage and increased family size have greater negative effects on annual earnings of the self-employed than on those of the organisational employed. The evidence indicates that at least part of the difference between the self-employed and organisational employed sectors is due to self-employed women making relatively greater reductions in the intensity of hourly work effort in response to increased household responsibilities.

Chitsike[29] (2000) examined the barriers to rural women entrepreneurship in Zimbabwean. The study indicated that Zimbabwean women's business tends to be small and are not supported by the legal system, which is based on male standards and language. In customary law women do not have individual economic rights, on the grounds that the benefits are given to them through their spouses or male relatives. The study suggested that it is exceptionally difficult for Zimbabwean women to become entrepreneurs: They will not do so unless there are challenges to culture. They will continue to regard themselves as secondary earners who do not have the responsibility of being breadwinners. They will remain trapped in small scale, low-investment business which can't lead to liberating economic empowerment that provides independence for men.

Ehelers and Karen[30] (1998) suggested that economic, socio cultural and gender constraints make it extremely difficult for most women to micro enterprises but viable income producers. Based on a research in a highly respected urban centre for women in the United States, the researcher argues that micro enterprise development is more detrimental and problematic than it is purported to be. Two reasons are isolated: At first gender constraints mean women tend to choose small- scale, under capitalized and barely profitable pink-collar businesses, largely home based operations based on work. Women are already doing a part of their gender specific role. Secondly micro enterprise training programmes reinforce this business segregation by discounting the socio cultural conditions women bring with them to business and instead emphasizes the personal growth of individuals. The result is that women are encouraged to maintain their economic vulnerability and social peripheralisation rather than become part of the mainstream business world.

Miri Lerner[31] (1997) Examined the factors in flounce performance of Israeli women owned business. The study had a sample of 200 women business owners. The demographic variables showed that the majority of Israeli women entrepreneurs are married and become entrepreneurs after their children were grown. This is consistent with the strong family orientation prevalent is the Israeli culture and the existence of Institutional arrangements. The results of the study further showed that network affiliation, motivation, human capital and environmental factors affected different aspects of performance where as social learning theory had no significant effect on performance outcomes.

A study (1997) has been conducted in Poland by Zapalska[32] to investigate whether the polish female entrepreneur's possess the characteristics required for effective performance of entrepreneurs. It was study found that masculine characteristics dominate the self-supported profile of these successful women entrepreneurs. They indicated their possession of aggressiveness, assertiveness, determination, strong leadership behaviours, highly developed communication skills, and analytical thinking. The study had also found that entrepreneurial women do that give greater weight to traditional feminine characteristics. The majority of women entrepreneurs were involved in business related to personal computer, consulting, sale and advertising. The study had found that most women had developed skills in previous employment, which they used intensively in the development stage of the firm. The most frequently mentioned areas of recent past experience were in the management of state owned enterprise and in programmeming, sales, administration, marketing and consulting.

Creevey's[33] (1996) study of micro enterprise project undertaken in Ghana surveyed women in five different villages, processing sea-nuts to make butter. The survey assessed their experience participating in micro enterprises development project that was aimed at converting some of their traditional processing techniques with more time efficient practices. When they were asked in interviews to tell about their experience with the project the women reported that their financial states had not significantly improved as a result of the new technology. The women reported that since they had adopted the new technology they had not been able to acquire any new assets. According to the study, the advancement in technology had not increased the market for sea butter and had not altered the prices the women could sell for it, but it had not allowed the women to reduce their workload as compared to when they employed the time intensive traditional practice.

Barbara[34] (1995) et.al analysed the role played by women in family business in rural China. The study further explored that why rural women are not predominating in small business sector. One speculative explanation, on the above question builds on possible differences in the history of agricultural and non-agricultural sidelines in the Maoist period. More over the finding of the study showed that men predominate in small family run businesses differ substantially for urban areas, where women are being moved out of secure state sector jobs and relegated to household-run businesses. The study concluded that in the area of household run businesses in rural China, men apparently lead the development and expansion of household business, while women increasingly specialize in agricultural activities.

Rahman Khan[35] (1995) analysed the entrepreneurial capacity of women in Bangladesh restaurant business. The study highlighted that there has been no real change in the condition of women in restaurant business. Although the women may have gained some mobility in the market place and they can now leave their homes to work in the restaurant, there is no change in terms of division of labour. In fact the restaurant business has increased the workload of women. The women themselves cannot visualize their future in terms of the restaurant enterprise, especially those whose husbands are involved. However women who are widowed, or separated try their best to establish the business for themselves, and may have the potential to develop into entrepreneurs. Thirdly, women's involvement in the restaurant generally makes no impact on the community in terms of increasing respect for women, or helping others.

Haynes[36] (1995) using data from the National Survey of Small Business Finance (NSSBF), examined the loan terms faced by women and men owned business to determine if there were gender differences in the cost of capital. He examined each loan type offered by each lender. While the mean values of interest rates appeared to differ, none of the comparisons reached statistical significance. The notion of the test revealed that women owned business pay higher interest rates than men-owned business, multivariate model controlling for credit risk, size, age, legal organisations, location, and financial market concentration was created, based upon this model, using all lenders and loans in a sample of 2302 business. Women owed business paid interest rates similar to men owned business but appeared to receive smaller loan amounts. He noted that women-owned business has a higher probability of resorting to non-institutional sources of financial capital, such as family and friends and a lower probability of acquiring mainstream types of financing such as line of credit loans.

Hisrich[37] (1994) analysed the nature of Hungarian women entrepreneurs and their role in the economy. He surveyed among fifty women entrepreneurs. In self assessing their personality traits, the Hungarian women entrepreneurs felt they were extremely energetic in social and high in terms of independence, self -dependence, anxious about work load. They now cook for longer hours or sometimes even several times a day. Secondly the women are increasingly dependent on them to work for the restaurants and goal-orientated. The three traits receiving a lower rating were competitive , idealistic and geniality. The study further stated that the women entrepreneurs in Hungary generally rated themselves low on all management skills – finance, marketing, innovation, operation and planning. The areas receiving the lower self-assessment were finance and marketing The major problem at start up were obtaining credit, weak collateral position and demands of company on personal relations. Other start up problem mentioned were lack of well organised market economy, shortage of working capital, and a short period of ownership.

Loscocco and Kevin's (1993)[38] investigated work- family connections and economic success of women and men as small business owners. The results of the study showed that gender similarity exists in the processes through which earnings are determined, although there are differences in the levels of many predictor variables. The women owners were not only more likely to be single than the men, they also spend more time on domestic duties, operate smaller and younger businesses and have less human capital. Further, family situation has a decided impact on these owners business success and thereby affects personal earnings given that business success strongly influences how large a salary owner takes from their business. The remaining gender gap in earnings results from male-female differences in business characteristics and human capital rather than from differences in these effects of these characteristics on business success (or) earnings.

Skinner[39] (1992) conducted a study in North Carolina in the USA on the female apparel entrepreneur in retail trade. The study showed that family affairs and lack of capital were seen as personal limitations hindering business success. Moreover previous experience and education were not the major reasons for choosing their apparel retail business. The study further explained that female retailers tended to be original founders of their business and were split between operating their business as a sole proprietorship or a corporation. The average number of employees was two, although over a third had no full time employees. The majority of females used a directive style of management and most of their experience was acquired in their own business. All respondents, except one, taken to the study consider profit as the main criterion with which they evaluate success.

Kalleberg & Leicht[40] (1991) analyzed how the survival and success of small business headed by men and women are related to industry differences organisational structures and attributes of owner operations. The results of the study indicated that companies headed by women were no more likely to go out of business than those headed by men. The processes generating survival did not differ by gender. The other effects were observed for only one gender. It showed that competition increased the death rate among businesses headed by women, and rapid changes in industrial population increased the survival chances of business headed by men. Moreover, the study explained the businesses headed by men had a higher level of gross earnings than those headed by women: mean earnings for the former were nearly $ 54,000 compared to about $ 46,000 for the latter.

Loscocco and Joyce[41] (1991) examined the status of small business ownership among women in United States. The study revealed that domestic responsibilities are likely to limit women's total commitment to their business. The authors provided evidence from the census data that while 60 per cent of women owners worked fewer than 29 hrs per week, only 41 per cent of male counterparts did so. Only 27 per cent of the women sampled devoted over 40 hrs per week to the business compared to 48 per cent of men. According to the study many women who own small business view marriage as a hindrance to their success in contrast to men who count on support from their spouses, particularly during start up. Many women pursue small business ownership because they have difficulty in balancing the constraints of working for someone else with their well documented domestic responsibility even though most such women share with similar men the desire to achieve personal and economic success as well.

Loscocco[42] (1991) inquired the relative disadvantage of women in small business success. The study explained that there are number of possible reasons for women's relative lack of financial success. These can be broadly categorized as a function of individual difference brought to the small business sector or differences in the businesses themselves. The effects of marital status on income suggest that the feminist stand of the gender's model's emphasis on family roles is important. These women are less successful than male counterparts not only because their business tend to be smaller but also because they do not derive as much financial benefit from size. While there is evidence that the business success levels of women would be much more comparable to those of men, if they had the same personal and business characteristics translates into less success among women than men. The study further investigated that, if women were to acquire the same structural position as men, they would generate $2,640,500 in sales. The figure represents an increase of $2,293,600 in sales volume achieve considerable less financial success than men, whose average was almost $3,500,000 in sales.

Colleratte and Aubrey[43] (1990) carried out two surveys in Quebec for analyzing socio economic evolution of women business owners. The second follow up study (1987) confirms the viability of female entrepreneurship indicated by the first (1986) study. Forty five per cent of the women surveyed were planning to expand in the coming two years, and only 9 per cent were considering giving up business or reducing the size of their business. The study further explained that the amount of personal income taken out of the business by women who have another job increased less than did the amount taken out by women who do not have another job 30 per cent vs 50 per cent increase in 1986 and a 46 per cent vs 66 per cent increase in 1987. Moreover 48 per cent of respondents reported having decreased the debt/equity ratio in 1986, where as 20 per cent increased it. It thus appears that the female entrepreneurs' attitude towards credit is that they want to reduce the level of debt as much as possible

Monica Belcourt[44] (1990) studied the successful Canadian female entrepreneurs on the assumption that the extreme sample would make more likely illustrate key factors. The result of the study indicated that there is an emphasis on self reliance, and indeed 67 per cent of this sample cited independence and control of their own destinies as the principal motivators for opening their own business. Of the 24 married women, 45 per cent felt that they could not rely on their husbands for diverse reasons, like couldn't keep a job (11%), lack of ambition (8%) alcoholism (6%) illegal affairs (6%), and business failures (6%). The indirect message from the traditional source of support was to rely on themselves, because others were unwilling or unable to support them. The study further disclosed that about 40 per cent of the entrepreneurs were unable to fit into the corporate world because of being fined or laid off (17%) employer discrimination (17%) or inability to find work (11%).

Nelson[45] (1989) investigated the relevance of significant others for the female business owner. A typology of attributes was developed from social interaction theories for use in categorizing results. The findings of the study revealed that the most frequently identified significant other was the female entrepreneur's spouse, followed by a male friend. Characteristics most often observed were had business skills the owner felt she lacked and had much general business and life experience. The study had also found that providing emotional support was the most frequently mentioned type of contribution followed by planning advice and day- today assistance and physical and financial support

Evans and Jovanovic[46] (1989) analysed the liquidity constraints of micro-enterprises in Mexico. The study highlighted that there is a positive relationship between the probabilities of starting a business, and obtaining a loan. The size of the owners personal assets is indicative of the existence of liquidity constraints in the credit markets. Secondly, when the owner's personal characteristics, the characteristics of micro enterprises, the sector of operations variable, the geographical region indicators, and the control for micro enterprise dynamics are tested for the existence of liquidity constraints in the Mexican formal credit sector, the results reinforce the existence of liquidity constraints at the time of obtaining start-up capital.

Neider[47] (1987) undertook a study of female entrepreneurs in order to investigate the personality characteristics of the female entrepreneur and the organisational patterns of their business. The study found that over one-third of the women had started their business because of a personal crisis (divorce, death of spouse etc). Reasons given by the other two thirds of the respondents for business start-up involved personal satisfaction issues. None of the females interviewed mentioned money as a primary motivator for starting a business. Regarding perceived strengths were high energy level and skill in influencing others are mentioned. The two major weaknesses mentioned were inability to delegate and personal life versus career tension.

Cromie[48] (1987) examined the motives that stimulate individuals into becoming business proprietors. Results based on personal interviews with 35 men and 34 women indicate that both genders do have a variety of reasons for founding and that women, as well as men, are primarily motivated by autonomy, achievement, a desire for job satisfaction and other non-economic rewards. The study revealed that male and female samples have similar scores on their needs for achievement and autonomy suggest that they possess the intrinsic personality traits that often lead to successful entrepreneurial behaviour. However, differences in matures: women are dissatisfied with their careers and see entrepreneurship as a means of accommodating their work and child rearing roles simultaneously while men are more strongly motivated by making money and have more experience of business founding that women.

Scott[49] (1986) conducted a study in Georgia, on both male and female entrepreneurs for the purpose of comparisons of gender. The objective of the study was to find out whether one's own business had been more profitable or difficult, or less profitable or difficult than expected. The result of the study showed that 48 per cent of women entrepreneurs were making more income than expected, whereas 28 per cent of male had the same. Similarly only 16 per cent of the women found running their own business to be more difficult, while 42 per cent of male found it be difficult. The women were more often surprised pleasantly or unpleasantly by the profitability of their business than were the men. 61 per cent of the men, but only 20 per cent of the women, found their profits to be close to what they have expected. On the other hand the women entrepreneurs were less often surprised by the difficulties resulting from entrepreneurship than men were.

Hisrich[50] (1984) analyzed the business problems and management skills of women entrepreneurs. The study indicated that nearly all the women entrepreneurs had encountered with their business during start-up and current operations. The biggest problems during start-up were lack of business and financial training and lack of collateral. The other cited problems were lack of education, experience in management, hiring competent staff and attracting customers, which were deemed relatively unimportant during start-up took on increased importance. After the introductory stage, the demands of the business impinging on personal life also appeared to become more of a problem.

INDIAN STUDIES

Bhagyavathi[51] et.al (2008) conducted a study in Chikkamangalur district in Karnataka to know the participation level of farm women in entrepreneurship activities of Self Help Groups. The study revealed that family size, training status and mass media participation of the farm women had no association with the participation level. On the other hand group leadership and farm status had highly significant association with participation level.

Rajani[52] (2008) analyzed and found out that twenty six per cent of female entrepreneurs received skills oriented business training, the remaining seventy four per cent did not receive any training. Only -eighteen per cent of women had undergone training before start up. Most of the women entrepreneur (94%) did not want to extent their business to other towns and cities. The reasons were that it may affect their families. It is almost impossible to expand the business because the markets for the type of products and services tend to be primarily local.

Poonam[53] et.al (2008) investigated the impact of motivational factors and role stress on women. The study was carried out in Jammu & Kashmir district taking up 240 respondents. It was found that liking for having an independent occupation (85%) ranked first among personal motivators followed by monotony of house work with the score of 77 per cent. The study explained that women were subjected to a greater stress as the demands of home and career at times caused conflict. The respondents adopted various strategies in resolving the contact stress. The mostly resolved them conflict by working on priorities (55%) followed by working harder (27%).The remaining respondents accepted the situation with the score of 11 per cent while 7 per cent of the respondents depended on their faith on god.

Shivani Sharma[54] (2008) conducted a study in Punjab to ascertain the prospects and problem of women entrepreneurs through SWOT analysis. The study showed that major threat as perceived by women entrepreneurs from all the enterprises were "burden of dual responsibility" which may be because burden of household as well as that of enterprise sometimes clashes and blocks their activities. The second major threat perceived by most of the respondents was "problems of power shut downs" but in case of direct marketing this problem was not seen, as their main work was done by the company only. Further the study showed that in all the enterprises women disagreed with the statement that shifting of business due to marketing problems was the threat to them. The least important threat felt by majority of the women was male dominance.

Femida Handy[55] et.al (2007) conducted a study in Maharashtra to look at the behaviour of women entrepreneurs in both profit and non- profit sectors and test the potential differences and similarities. The result indicated that neither the young children nor the presence of a husband affected women's decisions to start an enterprise (or) her choice of sector. However domestic responsibilities in some cases dissuaded entrepreneurs from taking an additional risk for essential growth. In the non-profit sector the human capital of parents shaped value of entrepreneurs that fuelled the interest and commitment while in the profit sector, the parental and spousal entrepreneurs influenced the women by encouraging them and providing them skills and experience for running a profit enterprise.

Pooja Nayyar[56] (2007) conducted a study in Himachel Pradesh to analyze the causes and constraints faced by women entrepreneurs in entrepreneurial process. The study had identified various constrains including financial, marketing, production and health problems faced by the women entrepreneur. During the process of marketing, they face poor location of shop, lack of transport facility and tough competition from larger and established units. With regard to problem of production, non availability of raw material was the biggest problem they face. Among the health problems, the respondents had tension, backache, eyestrain, and the problem of feeling fatigue after returning home. Causable factors were lack of rest and heavy schedule.

Spinter Dhaliwal[57] (2000) conducted study which focuses on the often – neglected issue of the contribution of Asian women to both entrepreneurship and the management of small business in order to illuminate the position of Asian women in business. A series of interview were undertaken with two particular groups. Asian women entrepreneurs in the own right, and the Asian women working in the family enterprises. This exploratory study suggests that there are distinctive issues faced by the South Asian women involved in small business and that their families can help or hinder them. What comes out of this study was not the differences between the personal characteristics of the women in the two groups, when their education and motivations are similar, but the crucial nature of the class position of the husband extended family.

For the independent women their higher position and outlook requires the women to look after the children and reinforce status. The hidden women, on the other hand, reproduce relations where domestic and marked relations are interwoven.

Ajit Kanitkar[58] (1994) examined the emergence of entrepreneurs of micro-enterprise in rural India. The result of the study had two peculiar aspects of the dynamics involved in the management of the 86 enterprises taken for the sample. Firstly there was a problem of debt recovery from the clients. To establish themselves in the village business environment, the new entrants began their operations by offering generous credit to their customers whether it was a manufacturing or a service unit. This was one reason why they got into the credit trap. The second problem which was peculiar to the management of the business was that of reaching a stage of maturity or saturation. The types of business which these entrepreneurs chose were mostly service industries, having very low value addition and few entry barriers.

Rao[59] (1991) identified the factors that impede and slow down the entrepreneurial development of rural women based on the response of random sample of 81 women enterprisers in Anantapur district of Andrapradesh. The finding showed that economic backwardness, lack of family and community support, ignorance of opportunities, lack of motivation, preference of traditional occupations and for seemed jobs were some of the factors that inhibit the promotion of grass root entrepreneurship among rural women.

Pillai and Anna[60] (1990) attempted to study women entrepreneurship in Kerala. The objective was to find out the social, political and economic factors that prevented entrepreneurship development. A randomly selected sample of 102 women entrepreneurs was surveyed. The study showed that entrepreneurs depended on financial support from the state and that financial assistance was used only as a secondary help. The respondents had cited that family support and encouragement as the highest facilitating factors for them to do business.

The studies some of which referred above assess the women entrepreneurs' profile, motivation, gender comparison in general. Therefore, there is a divergence of views and approaches in the study concept. Moreover, despite the relative importance of women entrepreneurship, there is paucity of literature of women micro enterprises in Tamilnadu. This exploratory study attempts to shed light on a number of issues faced by the self employed women in small business and micro enterprise sector.

REFERENCES

1. Ingoid Verheul, Martin Carree and Roy Thorik (2009) "Allocation and Productivity of Time in New Ventures of Female and Male Entrepreneurs" *Small Business Economics*, Vol. 33, No. 3, pp. 273-291.
2. Eshetu Bekele and Zelete Worku (2008) "Women Entrepreneurship in Micro Small and Medium Enterprises: The Case of Ethiopia", *Journal of International Women Studies*, Vol. 10, No. 2, November, pp. 3-18.
3. Adereni M.O, Liori H.O, Siyanbola W.O, Adegbite and Adebereijo S.A (2008) "An Assessment of the Choice and Performance of Women Entrepreneurs in Technological and Non-technological Enterprises in South Western Nigeria," *African Journal of Business Management*, Vol. 2, No. 10, October, pp. 165-176.
4. Muhammad Azam Roomi and Guy Parrot (2008) "Barriers to Development and Progression of Women Entrepreneurs in Pakistan" *The Journal of Entrepreneurship*, Vol. 17, No. 1, pp. 59-72.
5. Williams. D.A (2008) "Export Stimulation in Micro and Small Locally Owned Firms from Emerging Environments: New Evidence", *Journal of International Entrepreneurship*, Vol. 6, pp. 101-102.
6. Francis M.Hill, Claire M.Leitch & Richard M.Harrison (2006) "Desperately Seeking Finance? The Demand for Finance by Women Owned and Led business", *Venture Capital*, Vol. 8, No. 2, April. pp. 159-182.

7. Selvamalar Ayadurai M. Sadia Sohaul (2006) "Profile of Women Entrepreneurs in a War-torn Area. A Case Study of North East Sri Lanka", *Journal of Development Entrepreneurship*, Vol. 11, No. 1, pp. 3-17.

8. Luis M.Shellon (2006) "Female Entrepreneurs, Work-Family Conflict and Venture Performance: New Insights into the Work-Family Interface," *Journal of Small Business Management*, Vol. 44, No. 2, pp. 285-297.

9. Morris Michel H, Nola N. Miyasaki, Craig E.Watters, and Susam. M Coombes (2006) "The Dilemma of Growth: Understanding Venture Size Choices of Women Entrepreneurs", *Journal of Small Business Management*, Vol. 144, No. 2, pp. 221-241.

10. Heikki Haino (2006) "Use of Borrowed Start-up Capital and Micro Enterprise in Mexico. Existence of Liquidity Constraints", *Portuguese Economic Journal*, Vol. 5, No. 1, pp. 1-30.

11. Elizabeth Walker and Bererly Webster (2006) "Management Competencies of Women Business Owners," *Entrepreneurship Management*, Vol. 2, pp. 495-508.

12. Kathleen Dechant and Asya & L.Lanky (2005) "Toward an Understanding of Arab Women Entrepreneurs in Bahrain and Oman", *Journal of Development Entrepreneurship*, Vol. 10, No. 2, pp. 123-140.

13. Gray R.Kenneth and Joycelyn Finley Harvey (2005) "Women and Entrepreneurship in Morocco-Debunking Stereo Types and Discerning Strategies" *International Entrepreneurship and Management Journal*, Vol. 1, pp. 203-217.

14. Joan Winn (2005) "Women Entrepreneurs; Can We Remove the Barriers." *International Entrepreneurship and Management Journal*, Vol. 1, pp. 381-397.

15. Helen Ruth Appas (2004) "Minority Women's Micro Enterprises in Rural Areas of the United States of America, Africa American, Hespanic American and Native American Case Studies", *Geo Journal*, Vol. 61, pp. 281-289.

16. Alicia. M. Robb (2002) "Entrepreneurial Performance by Women and Minorities: The Case of New Firms", *Journal of Development Entrepreneurship*, Vol. 7, No. 4, December.

17. *Op.cit.*, Carlied Holm , pp. 227-242.

18. Gundry L.K. (2001) "The Ambitious Entrepreneurs: High Growth Strategies of Women Owned Enterprises", *Journal of Business Venturing*, Vol. 16, No. 4, September pp. 453-470.
19. Hatun Ufuk and "Ozen "Ozan (2001) " The Profile of Women Entrepreneurs". *International Journal of Consumer Studies"*, Vol. 25, No. 4, December, pp. 299-308.
20. Muriel Orhan (2001) "Women Business owners in France – The Issues of Financing Discrimination", *Journal of Small Business Management*, Vol. 39, No. 1, pp. 95-102.
21. Holy Buttner. E. "(2001) "Examining Female Entrepreneur's Management Style: An Application of a Relational Frame", *Journal of Business Ethics*, Vol. 29, pp. 253-269.
22. Lee M.A & Michel S. Rendell (2001) "Self-Employment Disadvantage in the Working Lives of Blacks and Females", *Population Research and Policy Review*, Vol. 20, pp. 291-320.
23. Ingoid Verheul and Roy Thorik (2001) "Start-up Capital "Does Gender Matter", *Small Business Economics*, Vol. 16, pp. 329-35.
24. Almas Heshmati (2001) "On the Growth of Micro and Small Firms; Evidence from Sweden", *Small Business Economics*, Vol. 17, pp. 213-228.
25. Alexandar L.Anna, Gayler N.Chandler,Erik Jansen, P.Mero (2000)"Women Business Owners in Traditional & Non Traditional Industries", *Journal of Business Venturing*, Vol. 15, No. 3, May, pp. 279-303.
26. Priscilla Chu (2000) "The Characteristics of Chinese Female Entrepreneurs: Motivation and Personality", *Journal of Enterprising Culture*, Vol. 8, No. 1, March pp. 67-84.
27. *Op.cit.*, Sherri Grasmuck and Rosario Espinal, pp. 231-255.
28. Greg Hundly (2000) "Male/Female Earning Differences in Self-employment: The Effects of Marriage, Children and the Household Division of Labour", *Industrial and Labour Relation Review*, Vol. 54, No. 1, October.
29. *Op.cit.*, Colletah Chitsike pp. 71-77.
30. Tracy Bachrach Ehlers and Karen Mein (1998) "Women and the False Promise of Micro Enterprise", *Gender and Society*, Vol. 12, No. 4, pp. 424-440.
31. Miri Lerner, Candida Brush & Rober Hirrich (1997) "Israeli Women Entrepreneurs: An Examination of Factors Affecting Performance", *Journal of Business Venturing*, Vol. 12, November-July, pp. 315-339.

32. Zapalska. A (1997)" A Profile of Women Entrepreneurs and Enterprises in Poland," *Journal of Small Business Management'* Vol. 35, pp. 76-82.

33. Creevey L"(1991)"*Changing Women's Lives and Work*", Intermediate Technology Publication, London, UK.

34. Barbara Entwisle, Gail E. Hendrson, Susan E.Short, Jill Bouma, Zhai Fengying (1995) "Gender and Family Business in Rural China", *American Sociological Review,* Vol. 60, February pp. 36-57.

35. Mahmuda Rahman Khan (1995) "Women Entrepreneurs in the Bangladeshi Restaurant Business", *Development Practice,* Vol. 5, No. 3, August pp. 240-246.

36. Haynes.G.W (1995) "*Executive Summary: Financial Structure of Women Owned Businesses* (SBA-8029-oA.93) Washington Dc: Small Business Administration.

37. Rebort D. Hisrich & Gyula Fulop (1994) "The Role of Women Entrepreneurs in Hungary's Transition Economy" *International Studies of Management & Organisation*, Vol. 24, No. 4, pp. 100-117.

38. Karyn. A.Loscocco and Kevin T.Leich (1993) "Gender Work-family Linkages and Economic Success Among Small Business Owners" *Journal of Marriage and Family,* Vol. 55, November, pp. 875-887.

39. Skinner D. Sandra (1992) Female Entrepreneurs in the Retail Trade: A Study of Personal and Professional Traits as they Impact on Business Environments", *The International Review of Retail Distribution and Consumer Research,* Vol. 2, No. 2, pp. 183-195.

40. Arne L. Kalleberg and Kevin.T Leicht (1991) "Gender and Organisational Performance: Determinants of Small Business Survival and Success", *Academy of Management Journal,* Vol. 34, No. 1, pp. 136-161.

41. Karyn. A. Loscocco and Joyce Robinson (1991) "Barriers to Women's Small Business Success in the United States" *Gender & Society,* Vol. 5, No. 4, December, pp. 511-532.

42. Loscocco K.A, Robinson A.J, Richard H. Hell and John. K. Allen (1991) "Gender and Small Business Success," *Social Force,* Vol. 70, No. 1, September, pp. 65-85.

43. Collerette. P and Aubry P. (1990) "Socio-economic Evolution of Women Business Owners in Quebec-1989", *Journal of Business Ethics*, Vol. 9, pp. 417, 422.

44. Monica Belcourt (1990) "A Family Portrait of Canada's Most Successful Female Entrepreneurs", *Journal of Business Ethics*, Vol. 9, pp. 435-438.

45. Nelson G.W (1989) "Factors of Friendship: Relevance of Significant Others to Female Business Owners", *Entrepreneurship Theory & Practice*, Vol. 13, No. 4, pp. 7-18.

46. Evans David. S. Jovanovic Boyan (1989) An Estimate Model of Entrepreneurial Choice under Liquidity Constraints", *Journal of Political Economy*, Vol. 97, No. 4, pp. 8008.

47. Neider. L (1987) "A Preliminary Investigation of Female Entrepreneur in Florida", *Journal of Small Business Management*, Vol. 25, No. 3. pp. 22-29.

48. Stanley Cromie (1987) "Motivations of Aspiring Male and Female Entrepreneurs", *Journal of Occupational Behaviour*, Vol. 8, pp. 251-261.

49. Carole E.Scoot (1986)" Why More Women are Becoming Entrepreneurs", *Journal of Small Business Management*, Vol. 24. No. 4, October pp. 37-50.

50. Robert. D. Hisrich & Candida Brush (1984)" The Women Entrepreneur Management Skills and Business Problem" *Journal of Small Business Management*, Vol. 22, No. 1, pp. 30-37.

51. Bhagyavathi, Venugopal.G, Nagesha and Naga Bhusam, (2008) "Participation Level of Farm Women in Entrepreneurship Under SHG's", *Mysore Journal of Agricultural Science*, Vol. 42, No. 1, pp. 159-162.

52. *Op.cit.*, Rajani N. (2008) pp. 277-281.

53. Poonam Parihar, Sing D.K, Sharma V.K. and Sing R.P. (2008). Impact of Motivational Factors and Role Stress on Women Entrepreneurs in Jammu", *Indian Research Journal of Extension Education*," Vol. 8, No. 2 & 3, pp. 73, 76.

54. Shivani Sharma & Gurprit Singh Dhillon (2008) "Identification of Prospects and Problems of Women Entrepreneurs of Punjab Through SWOT" *Indian Journal of Social Research*, Vol. 49 , No. 3, July-September, pp. 245-257.

55. Femida Handy, Bhagyashree Renade, Meena Kasam (2007) "To Profit to Non-profit -Women Entrepreneurs in India", *Non-profit Management and Leadership*. Vol. 17, No. 7, pp. 383-399.

56. Pooja Nayyar , Avinash Sharma, Jatinder Kishtwaria , Aruna Rana & Neena Vyas (2007)" Causes and Constraints Faced by Women Entrepreneurs in Entrepreneurial Process", *Journal of Social Science*, Vol. 14, No. 2, pp. 99-102.

57. Spinder Dhaliwal (2000) "Asian Female Entrepreneurs and Women in Business — An Exploratory Study " *Entrepreneurs and Women Management Studies* , Vol. 1, No. 2, pp. 207-216.

58. Ajit Kanitkar (1994) "Entrepreneurs and Micro-enterprises in Rural India "*Economic and Political Weakly*", Vol. xxix, No. 1, February.

59. Rao.C Hari Narayana (1991) "Promotion of Women Entrepreneurship, SEDME Journal, Vol. 18, No. 3, pp. 21-28.

60. Pillai N.C & V.Anna (1990) "The Entrepreneurial Sprit Among Women — A Study in Kerala", *Indian Management*. November-December, pp. 93-98.

3

Role of SHGs in Promoting Women Entrepreneurship

INTRODUCTION

The present chapter discusses the role of SHGs in promoting women entrepreneurship in Tamilnadu. The chapter is obvious, since the respondents of this study are the SHG members. The chapter is divided into three sections. The first part reviews the profile, trend and progress of SHGs in Tamilnadu. The second part discusses profile and progress of SHGs in the sample district. The third part explains the role of SHGs in entrepreneurial development of women.

SHG AND WOMEN EMPOWERMENT

Empowerment of rural women is one of the central issues in the developing countries all over the world. The empowerment of women can lead to bring a better society in the world. It provides power and makes them independent society builders with potential challenges to the future generation. Empowering the women at social, political and economical levels becomes necessary to convert the static society into a self-sustainable society. Women's active participation in economic activities leads to the economic development of a nation. The key area in empowerment of women is the economic area. Economic empowerment of women is fundamental to their overall empowerment. It implies a better quality of material life through sustainable livelihoods like micro enterprises governed by women.

Women empowerment can be achieved through policies of government, better education, raising employment of women and involvement of women in Self-Help Groups (SHGs). The formation of Self-Help Groups helps to improve the status of women in society and strengthen their economic status. The involvement of women in SHG leads to benefits not only to the individual but also to the family and community as a whole through collective action for development.

Concept and Origin of SHG

SHG is mainly concerned with the enlistment of the women in the society through social and economic aspects. It occupies the major part of the rural development of the nation, which constituted almost all parts of the nation. The concept was successfully implemented and achieved in Bangladesh. Later it has been introduced in India. Tamilnadu the southern state has become the prominent SHG constituted state in the country.

SHG is a small economically homogenous affinity groups of the rural poor voluntarily coming together to save small amount regularly, to be deposited in common fund known as Group Corpus. The members of the group agree to use this common fund and such other funds that they may receive as a group through a common management. The basic principles of the SHGs are group approach, mutual trust, organisation of small manageable groups, group cohesiveness, spirit of thrift, demand based lending, collateral free women friendly loan, skill training, capacity building, regular saving, periodic meeting, compulsory attendance and systematic training.

Generally a Self Help Group consists of 10 to 20 women members of the same socio-economic background residing in the same area to work together for their own upliftment. In case of areas with scattered and sparse population and difficult areas, like desert and hills, this number may be from 5 to 20. Generally all members of the group should belong to families below the poverty line. However if necessary, a maximum of 20 per cent and in exceptional cases, where essentially required, up to a maximum of 30 per cent of the member in a group may be taken from families, marginally above the poverty line, living contiguously with BPL families and if they are acceptable to the BPL members of the group. This would help the families of occupational groups like agricultural labourers, marginal farmers and artisans marginally above the poverty line or who may have been excluded from the BPL list to become members of SHG.

The group shall not consist of more than one member from the same family. A person should not be a member of more than one group. The group should devise a code of conduct (group management norms) to bind itself. This should be in the form of regular meetings (weekly or fortnightly), functioning in a democratic manner, allowing free exchange of views, participation by the members in the decision making process. The activities of the group are listed below:

- The group should draw up an agenda for each meeting and take up discussions as per the agenda.
- The members should build their corpus through regular savings. The group should be able to collect the minimum voluntary saving amount from all the members regularly in the group meeting. The savings so collected will be the group corpus fund.
- The group corpus fund should be used to advance loans to the members. The group should develop financial management norms covering the loan sanction, procedure, repayment schedule and interest rates.
- The members in the group should meet and take all the loaning decisions through a participatory decision making process.
- The group should be able to prioritize the loan applications, fix repayment schedules, fix approximate rate of interest for the loans advanced and closely monitor the repayment of the loan installment from the loan.
- The group should operate a group account preferably in their service area bank branch, so as to deposit the balance amount lift with the groups after disbursing loans to its members.

- The group should maintain simple basic records, such as minute's book, attendance register, loan ledger, general ledger, cash book, bank passbook and individual pass books.
- The members of the group elect one Animator and one Representative from the group to operate it.
- The role of these office bearers is to convene and conduct group meetings at regular intervals. Besides maintaining accounts and records, they should assist the group in getting bank loans, asset creation and coordinate with banks in the aspects of borrowing and repayment of loans.

SHG and Bank Linkage

There are three types of linkages between the banks and the SHGs. The first type is the relationship on the basis of commercial line. Under this activity, banks go to NABARD for refinance for the amount lent to the SHGs. This relationship is known as direct linkage.

The second scheme is based on the SGSY. Under this scheme SHGs avail revolving fund assistance from the banks to the tune of Rs. 25,000/- and this amount can be retained among the members till it is demanded. Banks charge interest only on the availed portion of the revolving fund assistance.

The third type is economic assistance programme, in which, based on the business promotion needs of the members, subsidy loan is sanctioned to the SHGs.

Trend and Progress of SHG in Tamil Nadu

In Tamil Nadu, the Self-Help Group movement was started in Dharmapuri District in the year 1989.It has now grown leaps and bounds covering all districts of the state targeting poor families and the marginalized sections of the society. The members and office bearers of the SHGs are promoted by Mahalir Thittam and they are provided systematic training to bring about qualitative changes in their attitude and promote cohension and effective functioning of the group. All the SHG members are imparted training in modules for four days. The primary objective of this training is to orient all members to the SHG concept and bring out the potentiality of all the members. The office bearers of SHGs (Animator and Representatives) are given training in modules for 6 days. The main objectives of this training are to enhance the leadership quality team building sprit and to build their capacity to maintain books of accounts. The number of group formations and the total savings of SHG members in Tamilnadu are presented in Table 3.1.

The Table 3.1 reveals the group formation and the number of women joined in SHG in Tamilnadu. The total groups formed in Tamilnadu are 4413317 and the number of women enrolled is 6,99,1366. Of which, the rural area accounted for 30, 2092 groups (68.45%) and the number of women is 4833472 (69.31%), whereas in urban area the number of groups formed are 139219 (31.54%) and the number of women are 2,15,7894 (30.82%). It shows that both the groups formed and the women enrolled are much higher in rural area than urban. It shows that the concept of SHG is effective role in empowering the women in rural Taminadu. The table also shows the district wise information. We understand Chennai district is ranked in first position, followed by Kancheepuram (23491 groups). Similarly the districts viz., Vilupuram, Trinelveli, Tiruvannamalai and Cuddalore have more women enrolled in SHGs.

The District wise information regarding savings of self help group members and loan obtained are presented in Table 3.2. As in Table 3.1 the savings amount is proportionally higher in rural than urban as the higher number self help groups are found in rural than urban. The table reveals that the total saving amount of self help group member is Rs 2,56,800.99 of which, the proportion of rural is 184342.92 (71.78%) and the urban was 74770.12 (29.11%). The table also exhibits the district wise figure, which also proves that the saving amount in all districts in rural is significantly higher than that of urban.

Table 3.1

District Wise-Group Formation of SHGs in Tamil Nadu

Sl.No.	Districts	Rural		Urban		Total	
		Groups Formed	Women Enrolled	Groups Formed	Women Enrolled		
01	Chennai	–	–	23620	366110	23620	366110
02	Coimbatore	9842	157472	5037	78073	14879	235545
03	Cuddalore	13890	222240	3815	59132	17705	281372
04	Erode	9456	151296	5975	92612	15431	243908
05	Kancheepuram	16457	263312	7034	109027	23491	372339
06	Madurai	9707	155312	4713	73051	14420	228363
07	Salem	10952	175232	7512	116436	18464	291668
08	Thiruvannamalai	14833	237328	2814	43617	17647	280945
09	Tirunelveli	11789	188624	7196	111538	18985	300162
10	Tanjavur	13415	214640	3893	60341	17308	274981
11	Tiruvallur	10560	168960	6168	95604	16728	264564

(Table Contd…)

Sl.No.	Districts	Rural		Urban		Total	
		Groups Formed	Women Enrolled	Groups Formed	Women Enrolled		
12	Thoothukudi	10796	172736	4242	65751	15038	238487
13	Trichy	10415	166640	4915	76182	15330	267390
14	Vellure	13653	218448	2835	43942	16488	262390
15	Villupuram	16841	269456	2688	41664	19529	311120
	Other districts	129486	2071776	46762	724814	176248	2772022
	Total	302092	4833472	139219	2157894	441311	6991366

Source: Mahalir Thittam, as on March 2009

Table 3.2

District Wise Saving Details of SHGs

Sl.No.	Districts	Savings		Total
		Rural	Urban	
01	Chennai	-	9948.75	9948.75
02	Coimbatore	5022.78	3502.40	8525.18
03	Cuddalore	81 22.87	2171.52	10294.39
04	Erode	5758.05	3186.70	8944.75
05	Kancheepuram	9342.66	3744.41	13087.07
06	Kaniyakumari	5062.41	6855.79	11918.20
07	Karur	7984.67	3841.53	11826.20
08	Krishnagiri	8562.00	230.80	8792.80
09	Madurai	6659.31	1854.50	8513.81
10	Nagapattinam	7340.93	1589.52	8930.45
11	Namakkal	5773.94	3161.31	8935.25
12	Tirunelveli	5825.63	4033.97	9859.60
13	Tanjavur	8168.70	1933.40	10102.10
14	Vellure	3497.77	302.69	9358.56
	Other Districts	97221.20	28412.83	117763.88
	Total	184342.92	74770.12	256800.99

Source: Mahalir Thittam, Govt of Tamil Nadu

SELF-HELP GROUPS IN COIMBATORE DISTRICT

Coimbatore is in existence since the year 1200 AD known as Chera Kingdom. The District is estimated around 11 degree in North latitude, 77 degree East Longitude and 43200 meters above mean sea level in the western part of Tamilnadu, India. The district in its present form was formed by bifurcating the erstwhile composite District into Coimbatore and Erode districts in 1979 retaining Coimbatore as its head quarters. The district is densely populated with 42.72 lakh, which include 2176031 male and 2095825 female as its populations. According to the 2001 census, the population per sq.km was 7469. The district is well known as "The Manchester" of South India because of its well-developed textile industry and other industrial base. The economy of the district depends predominantly on the small and cottage industries. The dry belt of the Coimbatore region comprises black cotton soil, which is suitable for cotton cultivation. This is the root cause of large-scale growth of textile mills ranging from small medium to the large sector.

The self help groups play a significant role in uplifting the socio-economic status of women in both rural and urban area of this district. Coimbatore is one among the largest districts having high number of self help groups in Tamilnadu. At present 15,651 groups are working with 2,21,674 women members. Of the total groups and women enrolled, the urban self help groups are relatively higher than that of the rural self help groups. The rural self help groups are found higher for less than four years of age group of self help groups, whereas the urban self help group is comparatively for above 4 years of age group.

ROLE OF SELF-HELP GROUPS IN PROMOTING WOMEN MICRO ENTERPRISES

The Self-help group's involvement in self-employment activities contributes to individual entrepreneurship and group entrepreneurship at the grass root level offers an opportunity for acquiring managerial skills and enhancing the income of the women rural poor. The individual or group entrepreneurship through self help group is considered to be an investment in the process of socio-economic development.

The micro credit mechanism of the self-help groups makes the member to involve in income generating activities. With the support of self help group, the rural women are engaged in small business and starting micro enterprise through which they are economically empowered.

Table 3.3

Block Wise Self-Help Groups in Coimbatore District

As on July 2010

Sl. No.	Name of the Block	Age Group (Years)							Total Women Covered	Total Savings in (crore)
		0-6 Months	6M-1 yr.	1-2	2-3	3-4	4+	Total		
I	Rural SHGs									
1.	Karamadai	24	34	115	20	21	830	1044	14844	5.10
2.	Pollachi North	17	22	8	0	159	661	867	12359	4.08
3.	Annur	21	0	103	0	0	617	741	10647	4.63
4.	Pollachi south	20	0	20	24	186	445	695	9990	3.31
5.	Anaimalai	10	36	37	43	90	402	618	8652	5.65
6.	Perinaikenpal-ayam	39	1	50	45	62	398	595	8486	5.41
7.	Sulur	47	0	43	21	34	350	495	7229	3.38
8.	Kinathukadavu	14	0	0	0	0	438	452	6510	1.49

(Table Contd…)

Sl. No.	Name of the Block	Age Group (Years)							Total Women Covered	Total Savings in (crore)
		0-6 Months	6M-1 yr.	1-2	2-3	3-4	4+	Total		
9.	Sultanpet	59	17	40	28	39	216	399	5820	0.70
10.	Thondamuthur	0	0	0	0	0	287	287	4018	8.04
11.	Sarkar Samukulam	9	0	0	0	4	157	170	2497	1.74
12.	Madukkarai	0	0	0	0	58	106	164	2296	21.97
	Sub Total (1+12)	260	110	416	181	653	4907	6527	93348	65.50
II	**Urban SHGs**									
A	Town Panchayat	47	23	69	112	209	3168	3628	50792	Na
B	Municipalilty	31	86	57	0	75	1898	2147	30648	Na
C	Corporation	25	156	264	116	608	2180	3349	46886	26.44
	Sub Total (a+b+c)	103	265	390	228	892	7246	9124	128326	Na
III	**Grand Total (I+II)**	363	375	806	409	1545	12153	15651	221674	–

Source: District Collectorate, Project Implementation Unit, Mahalir Thittam, Coimbatore 2010.

Depending on number of factors ranging from landholdings, subsidiary occupations, agro climatic conditions and socio-personal characteristics of the rural women and their family members, the areas of micro-enterprise also differ from place to place. The small business and micro enterprises started by the rural women are classified under three major heads:

1. Micro-enterprise development related to agriculture and allied agricultural activities: like cultivating organic vegetables, flowers oilseeds, and seed production, mushroom growing, beekeeping. Some other areas are dehydration of fruits and vegetables, canning or bottling of pickles, jams, squashes, dairy and other products that are ready to eat.
2. Micro-enterprise development related to livestock management activities: like dairy farming, poultry farm, livestock, feed production and production of vermin composting using the animal waste.
3. Micro-enterprise development related to household based operations like knitting, stitching, weaving, bakery and flour milling, petty shops, food preparation and preservation etc.

REFERENCES

1. Government of Tamil Nadu, (2010), Official Records Maintained by Project Implementation Unit, Mahalir Thittam, District Collector Office, Coimbatore, 2010.
2. Government of Tamil Nadu, (2010), Scheme on Mahalir Thittam by the Tamil Nadu Corporation for Development of Women Ltd., Ministry of Rural Development, Chennai.

4

Issues of Women Entrepreneurship in Small Business and Micro Enterprises

The fourth chapter focuses on the results based on the analysis of data collected from the sample respondents through sample survey conducted for this research work. The results have been presented in the form of frequency tables, cross tables with suitable statistics like percentages, factor analysis and reliability analysis. For a better understanding of the findings, the chapter is divided into eleven major headings such as demographic and enterprise profile of entrepreneur, motivational factor for business, issues in start-up and running the enterprise, issues related to marketing, loan, skill acquisition, success level and future aspiration of entrepreneur, cross tabulation analysis and statistical analysis . All these analyses have been carried out across the field of activities of women entrepreneurs in small business and micro enterprises viz:

- *Trade* which includes sale of Handicrafts, Textile and Fabric Shops, Readymade Home Appliances, Sale of Leather Products etc.;
- *Manufacturing* which includes Coirmaking, Candle-making, Bakery Products, Handicrafts, Herbal and Palm Products etc.; and
- *Service* which is related to Catering, Beauty Parlors, Tailoring etc.

The discussion has been done in a concise manner keeping the objectives in focus.

DEMOGRAPHIC AND ENTERPRISE PROFILE OF WOMEN ENTREPRENEURS

The demographic factors such as age, educational qualification, and marital status are repeatedly reported to strongly influence self employment of women.

Table 4.1

Distribution of Respondents on the Basis of Age

Sl. No.	Category of Age		Trade	Manufac-turing	Service	Total
1.	>30	Frequency	3	4	2	9
		%	1.3	3.2	2.2	2.0
2.	31 to 40	Frequency	108	66	46	220
		%	46.2	52.4	51.1	48.9
3.	41 to 50	Frequency	102	47	34	183
		%	43.6	37.3	37.8	40.7
4.	Above 50	Frequency	21	9	8	38
		%	9.0	7.1	8.9	8.4
	Total	Frequency	234	126	90	450
		%	100.0	100.0	100.0	100.0

It could be observed from the table 4.1 that nearly 49 per cent of the women entrepreneurs are in the age group between 31 and 40 which is next to nearly 41 per cent women in the group of age 41-50. A minimum per cent of respondents (8.4%) are above 50. Similarly only 2 per cent of the sample respondents age is less than 30. It can be concluded that majority of the respondents are between the age groups 31 to 40 and 41 to 50.

Table 4.2

Distribution of the Respondents by Community

Sl. No.	Category of Community		Trade	Manufac-turing	Service	Total
1.	Backward class	Frequency	145	87	69	301
		%	62.0	69.0	76.7	66.9
2.	Most backward class	Frequency	18	4	2	24
		%	7.7	3.2	2.2	5.3
3.	SC/ST	Frequency	60	29	17	106
		%	25.6	23.0	18.9	23.6
4.	Others	Frequency	11	6	2	19
		%	4.7	4.8	2.2	4.2
	Total	Frequency	234	126	90	450
		%	100.0	100.0	100.0	100.0

It is observed from the table 4.2, with regard to the category of community of the respondents, a vast majority (67%) belong to backward class, of which the respondents in service business are found to be the (76.7%) highest. Next to it are the respondents of SC/ST community of respondents who account for 24 per cent. Among the SC/ST community the category of trade (25.6%) is the highest. The table further explains that 5.3 per cent belong to most backward class and only 4.2 per cent belong to the other (FC) community. It is interpreted that the highest numbers of sample respondent belong to the backward class.

It could be observed from the table 4.3 nearly 94 per cent of respondents are Hindus. A small proportion (0.7% Christian), (5.8% Muslim) belongs to the other religions.

Table 4.3

Distribution of Respondents According to Religion

Sl. No.	Religion		Trade	Manufac-turing	Service	Total
1.	Hindu	Frequency	218	117	86	421
		%	93.2	92.9	95.6	93.6
2.	Christian	Frequency	2	1	0	3
		%	.9	.8	.0	.7
3.	Muslim	Frequency	14	8	4	26
		%	6.0	6.3	4.4	5.8
	Total	Frequency	234	126	90	450
		%	100.0	100.0	100.0	100.0

Table 4.4

Distribution of Respondents According to Marital Status

Sl. No.	Marital Status		Trade	Manufac-turing	Service	Total
1.	Married	Frequency	218	120	86	414
		%	93.16	95.22	95.55	94.22
2.	Divorce separated	Frequency	13	6	2	21
		%	5.55	4.76	2.22	4.67
3.	Widow	Frequency	3	0	2	5
		%	1.28	.0	2.22	1.11
	Total	Frequency	234	126	90	450
		%	100.0	100.0	100.0	100.0

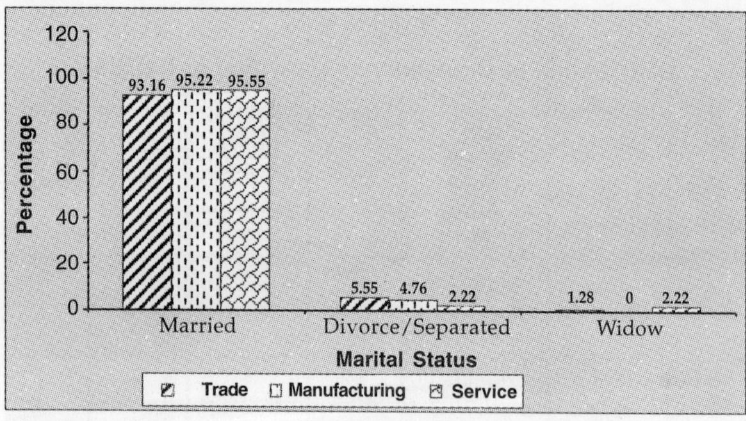

Fig. 4.1: Percentage Distribution of Respondents by Marital Status

Since the effect of marriage of female's relative earnings is likely to be much greater for the self-employed than other source of earnings, it is less constrained in the allocation of efforts between house work and business work. It is found that 92 per cent of the respondents are married women and living within the common law. Next to it 4.66 per cent are married but not living within the common law, that they might have been either separated or divorced women. The remaining 1.11 per cent of the women is widows. It has also been understood from the table that spinsters are not found in the present study.

The family structure in terms of the number of family members is one of the variables strongly affecting the decision of a woman in choosing self-employment. It has been found that from the above table 4.5, a vast majority of the respondent's family size consists of four to six members, whereas almost all the categories of business have got the similar proportion. Nearly 10 per cent of respondents' family consists of members above six.

Table 4.5

Distribution of Respondents on the Basis of Number of Family Members

Sl. No.	Number of Family Members		Trade	Manufac-turing	Service	Total
1.	Upto three	Frequency	29	10	5	44
		%	12.4	7.9	5.6	9.8
2.	Four to six	Frequency	196	112	81	389
		%	83.8	88.9	90.0	86.4
3.	Above six	Frequency	9	4	4	17
		%	3.8	3.2	4.4	3.8
	Total	Frequency	234	126	90	450
		%	100.0	100.0	100.0	100.0

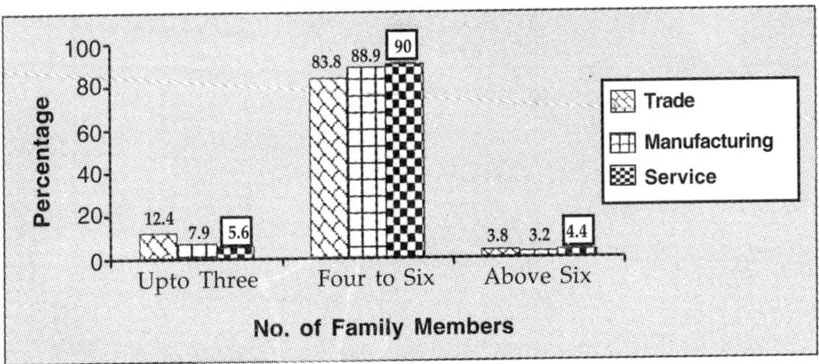

Fig. 4.2: Percentage Distribution of Respondents on the Basis of Number of Family Members

Educational level of women is a strong predicting factor of participation in self employment. Although education is not essential or mandatory for venture creations especially in small business, it does provide one with the skills, contacts, communication and opportunities, which are vital for a successful business.

Table 4.6

Distribution of Respondents by Educational Qualification and Category of Community

Sl. No.	Educational Qualification/ Community		BC	MBC	SC/ST	Others	Total
1.	Illiterates	Frequency	16	0	36	0	52
		%	5.3	.0	34.0	.0	11.6
2.	Primary School level	Frequency	173	11	65	9	258
		%	57.5	45.8	61.3	47.4	57.3
3.	High school level	Frequency	91	11	4	8	114
		%	30.2	45.8	3.8	42.1	25.3
4.	Higher secondary level	Frequency	15	2	1	2	20
		%	5.0	8.3	.9	10.5	4.4
5.	Degree/Diploma Holders	Frequency	6	0	0	0	6
		%	2.0	.0	.0	.0	1.3
	Total	Frequency	301	24	106	19	450
		%	100.0	100.0	100.0	100.0	100.0

Table 4.6 compares the educational level and different category of respondents of different communities. The justification for resorting to this comparison is that one can understand the women entrepreneurs of which community has obtained the lowest level and the highest level of education. It is found that majority of the respondents (57.3%) have completed only up to primary school level. As many as (25.3%) respondents have stepped out of primary school and completed high school education. It has also been found that 11.6 per cent have not enrolled even at the primary school

level. Only 4.4 per cent have got higher secondary education. Similarly the lowest percentage of women entrepreneurs are (1.3%) degree or diploma holders. It can be inferred that the educational status of the respondents of the study is generally low.

Table 4.7

Distribution of Respondent According to Occupational Background of Family

Sl. No.	Occupational Background		Trade	Manufac-turing	Service	Total
1.	Professional	Frequency	3	2	1	6
		%	1.28	1.58	1.11	1.3
2.	Business	Frequency	58	42	11	111
		%	24.78	33.33	12.22	24.7
3.	Labour in farm/ Non-farm activities	Frequency	117	43	45	205
		%	50.0	34.12	50.0	45.6
4.	Farmer	Frequency	56	39	33	128
		%	23.93	30.95	36.67	28.4
	Total	Frequency	234	126	90	450
		%	100.0	100.0	100.0	100.0

The Table 4.7 explains that 46 per cent of the respondents' family backgrounds are the labourers of farm and non-farm activities. Next to it, 28 per cent of respondents' family has got the background of agricultural farming. It is clearly understood that the family background of the entrepreneurs under studying is traditional and have low supplementing income. It further explains that 24.7 per cent are hailing from the business background, whilst only 1.3 per cent comes from professional families.

Past work experiences and events in the women's life are linked to their business practices. The previous occupational background plays a significant role in business success as it greatly influences the entrepreneurial venture by which the entrepreneur is able to bring all his knowledge and experience into the new direction of business.

Table 4.8

Distribution of Respondents on the Basis of Occupation before Entrepreneurship

Sl. No.	Nature of Occupation		Trade	Manufac-turing	Service	Total
1.	Housewife	Frequency	121	54	35	210
		%	51.7	42.9	38.9	46.7
2.	Student	Frequency	5	0	0	5
		%	2.1	.0	0	1.1
3.	Employee/labourer in farms/companies	Frequency	94	70	53	217
		%	40.2	55.6	58.9	48.2
4.	Family Business	Frequency	14	1	0	15
		%	6.0	.8	.0	3.3
5.	Social worker	Frequency	0	1	2	3
		%	.0	.8	2.2	.7
	Total	Frequency	234	126	90	450
		%	100.0	100.0	100.0	100.0

A majority of the respondents were employed (48.2%) in different organisations before stepping into small business or micro enterprises. Similar proportions of women (46.7%) are housewives and they declared that self help group formation has helped them to establish the micro enterprises. Only a few per cent of respondents (1.1% student), (0.7% social worker) (3.3% family business) are found to be in the other category of earlier occupations. It has been found out from the above table that the previous experience of the respondents was being employees in any kind of organisation or housewives.

Table 4.9

Distribution of Respondents on the Basis of the Duration of Ownership of Business

Sl. No.	Owner of Business		Trade	Manufac-turing	Service	Total
1.	< One year	Frequency	8	0	0	8
		%	3.4	.0	.0	1.8
2.	Two to three years	Frequency	56	45	29	130
		%	23.9	35.7	32.2	28.9
3.	Three to five years	Frequency	59	48	41	148
		%	25.2	38.1	45.6	32.9
4.	> Five years	Frequency	111	33	20	164
		%	47.4	26.2	22.2	36.4
	Total	Frequency	234	126	90	450
		%	100.0	100.0	100.0	100

It could be observed that with regard to the years of ownership of the respondents, the highest number of respondents (36.4%) started and carried their ventures for more than five years, of which activities of trade (47.4%) are higher than the other two fields like manufacturing and service activities. Nearly 33 per cent of the women entrepreneurs year of business runs up to three to five years, of which respondents of service business accounting 45.6 per cent is relatively higher than the other two activities. It is followed by 29 per cent of the respondent's years of business running for two to three, of which, the activity of manufacturing (35.7%) is found to be higher than the respondents of trade and service activities. Only 1.8 per cent of respondents have started and run their business for less than one year. It can be interpreted that the majority of the respondents' experience of the concerned business is at the level of two to five years.

Table 4.10

Distribution of Respondents According to the Location of the Business

Sl. No.	Location of the Business		Trade	Manufac-turing	Service	Total
1.	Own house	Frequency	136	76	52	264
		%	58.1	60.3	57.8	58.7
2.	Stall at the market	Frequency	42	33	26	101
		%	17.9	26.2	28.9	22.4
3.	Shop specifically allotted for business	Frequency	43	14	10	67
		%	18.4	11.1	11.1	14.9
4.	Land specifically allotted for business	Frequency	3	2	2	7
		%	1.3	1.6	2.2	1.6
5.	Others	Frequency	10	1	0	11
		%	4.3	.8	.0	2.4
	Total	Frequency	234	126	90	450
		%	100.0	100.0	100.0	100.0

Several of the location variables prove significant by having influenced the success of the business. It is a common observation that the location of this micro enterprise is the women's house since the investment level is low and modest.

The Table 4.10 also establishes the truth that nearly 59 per cent of the respondents are doing their business in their own house, wherein all the three categories of activities have the equal proportion (nearly 60%). Because of their domestic responsibilities, many women entrepreneurs need their business to be at their own home. Even these domestic responsibilities can drain their available time for business. But they can easily manage the family responsibilities even if they had gone for a rented stall or building. However going

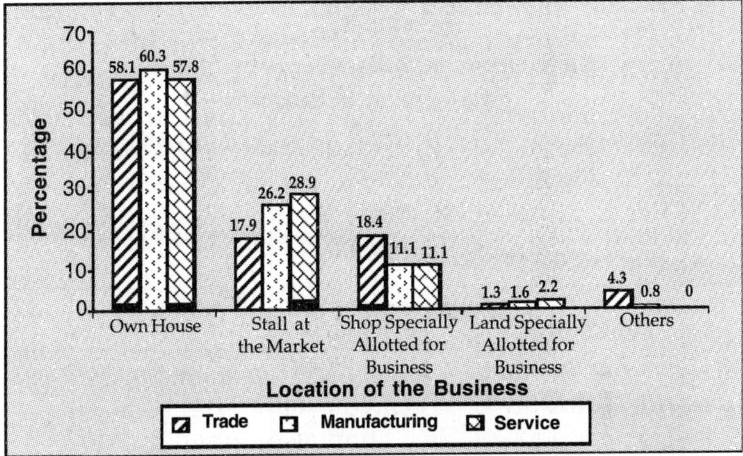

Fig. 4.3: Percentage Distribution of Respondents According to the Location of the Business

for a rented stall forces them to have additional financial burden. Next to it, 22.4 per cent of the respondent's locations are stalls in the market. It is also found that the other locations such as shop specifically allotted and land specifically allotted for business are not found to be significant. Only a meager percentage such as 15 per cent and 1.6 per cent do the business in such places. It can be concluded that the location for doing business is the biggest problem and many women entrepreneurs do their business mainly in their own house which may limit their opportunities to expand the business further.

One of the important roles for small and micro enterprises is to give gainful employment to the poor and downtrodden people since the nature of this work is traditionally associated with higher labour intensive techniques. Since the micro enterprises have relatively higher proportion of unskilled workers, creation of such unskilled jobs certainly has got a direct impact on the alleviation of poverty. However, owing to their minimum level of investment, normally they do not require more hiring labourers, as it is assisted mainly by the family members.

Table 4.11

Distribution of Respondents by Size of Employment in Business

Sl. No.	Size of Employment		Trade	Manufac-turing	Service	Total
1.	Only self	Frequency	118	62	45	225
		%	50.4	49.2	50.0	50.0
2.	One to three employees	Frequency	12	4	2	18
		%	5.1	3.2	2.2	4.0
3.	More than three employees	Frequency	8	3	1	12
		%	3.4	2.4	1.1	2.7
4.	Assisted by family members/Relatives	Frequency	96	57	42	195
		%	41.0	45.2	46.7	43.3
	Total	Frequency	234	126	90	450
		%	100.0	100.0	100.0	100.0

It could be observed from the table 4.11 that nearly 50 per cent of the respondents, included in all the three categories of business, are doing the business individually without the support of anyone. Next to it, 43.3 per cent of the women entrepreneurs are assisted by their family members. Both of these two categories of respondents have no hired employees. Only 4 per cent of the respondents employ one to three hired workers. It further shows that 2.7 per cent have employed more than 3 hired workers. It can be interpreted that the employment opportunity in these ventures is found to be minimal.

Although at the grass root level, micro enterprises need less fixed investment at the initial stage, the availability of the required fund for the enterprise is considered to be a positive factor for the women entrepreneurs. The traditional idea relies heavily on the proposition that creation and development of entrepreneurial talent largely depends on the adequacy of funds with the entrepreneur.

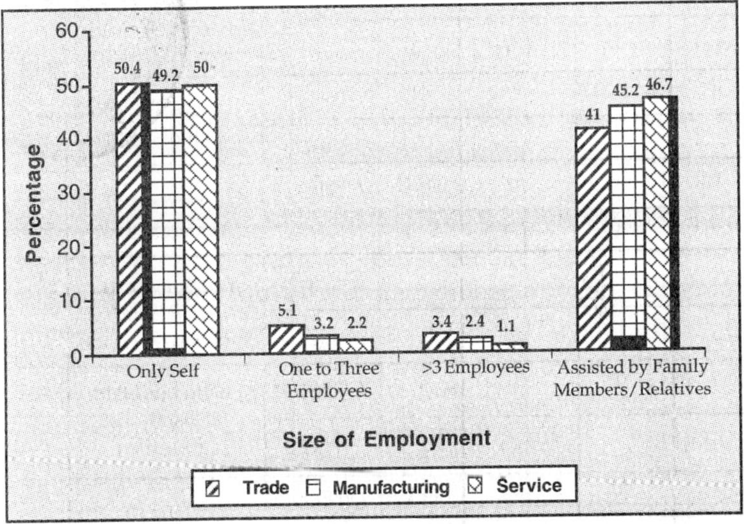

Fig. 4.4: Percentage Distribution of Respondents by Size of Employment in Business

It is found that a vast majority of the respondents invested a smaller amount in the business. Nearly 89 per cent of the respondents' initial investment is found to be less than one lakh. As against this, 6.22 per cent respondents have invested high amount exceeding Rs 10 lakhs at the time of start up. The remaining 2.88 per cent of the respondents have invested between one to five lakhs and five to ten lakhs respectively.

Entrepreneurs usually require financial assistance of some kind to launch their ventures. Be it formal bank loan or funds from their own savings, it is a common belief that women entrepreneurs in the traditional business have little access to funds to start their business ventures. The table 4.13 reveals the respondent's various sources of start -up capital for the business.

Table 4.12

Distribution of Respondents According to Initial Investment in Business

Sl. No.	Amount of Investment		Trade	Manufacturing	Service	Total
1.	Less than one lakh	Frequency	225	93	78	396
		%	96.15	73.8	88.8	88.8
2.	Rs. 1 lakh to 5 lakhs	Frequency	2	8	3	13
		%	0.8	6.34	3.3	2.88
3.	Rs. 5 lakhs to 10 lakhs	Frequency	3	7	3	13
		%	1.3	5.55	3.3	2.88
4.	Above 10 lakhs	Frequency	4	18	6	28
		%	1.7	14.28	6.6	6.22
	Total	Frequency	234	126	90	450
		%	100.0	100.0	100.0	100.0

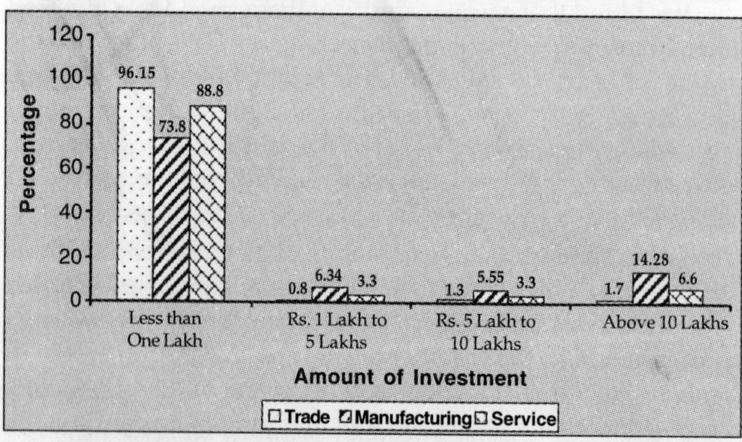

Fig. 4.5: Percentage Distribution of Respondents According to Initial Investment in Business

Table 4.13

Distribution of Respondents by Sources of Start-Up Capital

Sl. No.	Sources of Start-up Capital		Trade	Manufac-turing	Service	Total
1.	Savings by the respondents and support of family	Frequency	69	15	11	95
		%	29.5	11.9	12.2	21.1
2.	Finance by SHG only	Frequency	42	22	14	78
		%	17.9	17.5	15.6	17.3
3.	Both savings and SHG finance	Frequency	118	89	65	272
		%	50.4	70.6	72.2	60.4
4.	Borrowing from bank and SHG and one's own savings	Frequency	4	0	0	4
		%	1.7	.0	.0	.9
5.	SHG and other Non-financial Institutions	Frequency	1	0	0	1
		%	.4	.0	.0	.2
	Total	Frequency	234	126	90	450
		%	100.0	100.0	100.0	100.0

The source of finance of the women entrepreneurs for starting the business consists of their own savings, loan from concerned Self-Help Groups and borrowing from banks. The table shows that 21 per cent of the women entrepreneurs have raised their seed capital from their own savings and the financial support of immediate family members. A vast majority of the respondents have started the business with their savings along with the financial support of the concerned SHGs. Next to it, 17.3 per cent have started their ventures with the support of SHGs only. Only one per cent of the respondents resort to finance from banks at the time of launching their venture.

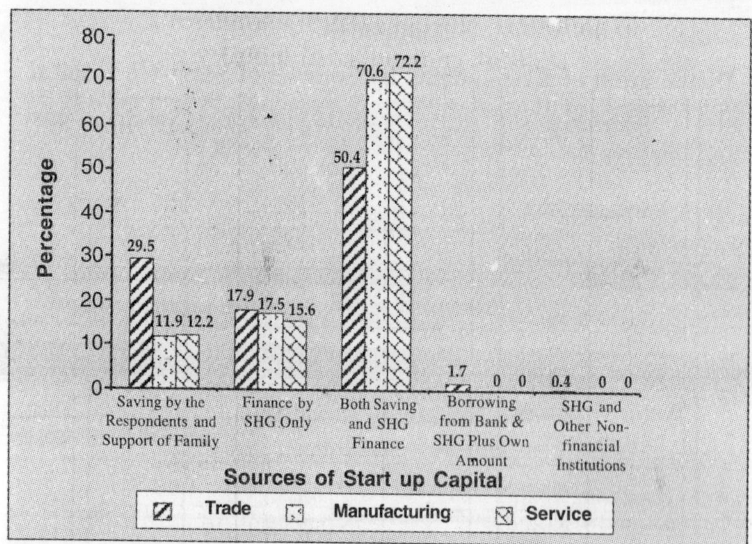

Fig. 4.6: Percentage Distribution of Respondents by Sources of Start-Up Capital

BACKGROUND INFORMATION OF BUSINESS AND MOTIVATIONAL FACTORS FOR SMALL BUSINESS AND MICRO ENTERPRISES

The following tables 4.14 and 4.15 explain the aspects of motivational factors for starting the venture. Idea for starting the new ventures would seem to be an important determinant for starting the business of the aspirants, as they would desire to get rich or meet challenges of life successfully.

It could be understood that as much as (82%) of respondents have been given idea/advice by the respective family members. Next to it 7.8 per cent of the respondents were doing the business using their property and their belongings. Less proportions of women entrepreneurs have started the enterprise/business by the recommendation of women SHGs' (8%). The other respondents have been given the idea by getting a brief account of the success stories of other female entrepreneurs (0.2%) and other factors (1.8%).

It can be concluded that the respondents have started their business with the support of family members' advice or motivation.

Table 4.14

Distribution of Respondents by Sources Providing Idea for Starting the Business

Sl. No.	Idea Given for Starting the Business		Trade	Manufac-turing	Service	Total
1.	Advice from family	Frequency	180	111	78	369
		%	76.9	88.1	86.7	82.0
2.	Inherited property	Frequency	19	8	8	35
		%	8.1	6.3	8.9	7.8
3.	Success stories	Frequency	1	0	0	1
		%	.4	.0	.0	.2
4.	SHG's recommendation	Frequency	31	4	2	37
		%	13.2	3.2	2.2	8.2
5.	Others	Frequency	3	3	2	8
		%	1.3	2.4	2.2	1.8
	Total	Frequency	234	126	90	450
		%	100.0	100.0	100.0	100.0

Motivational factors are considered to be very important in all theoretical models of entrepreneurial performance. It is necessary to identify what drives a woman to initiate, organise and manage the responsibilities for a business, which is challenging itself. Economic aspirations are crucial for entrepreneurs especially to small business enterprises and it is essential that one should understand the underlying motives for starting a business. Entrepreneurial motivation consists of both push and pulls factors. Push theory argues that individuals are pushed into entrepreneurship by negative external factors like his/her job dissatisfaction, difficulty in finding job, insufficient salary (or) inflexible job hours. Pull theory suggests that individuals are attached to entrepreneurial activity to seek total independence, self fulfillment and other desirable outcomes. There are ten motivational factors opted for choice. The respondents were asked to choose the main motivational factor and the reason to choose this particular business. The objective of this assessment is to find out the most important factor for motivation. Among the ten motivational factors three emerged as high as others. They are making money and profit (31.3%), self-reliance (30.7%) and self achievement (25.1%). The least important motivational factors are threat of losing the job (1.1%), family circumstance (0.4%), giving employment to others (0.4%), and owning a business of one's own (0.4%).

It could be concluded that there are different motivations for starting the business as per this study. Some women deliberately start the business as a means of supplementing income, while others eagerly anticipate individual achievement obtained from self employment.

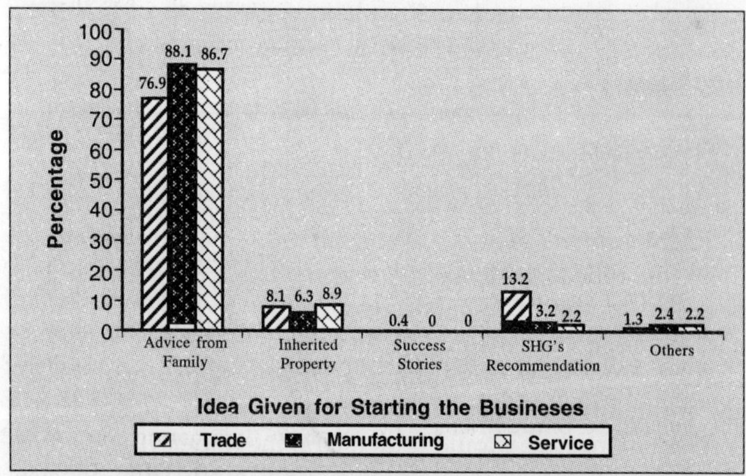

Fig. 4.7: Percentage Distribution of Respondents by Sources Providing Idea for Starting the Business

Table 4.15

Distribution of Respondents with Major Motivational Factors for the Business

Sl. No.	Motivational Factors with Nature of Business wise		Trade	Manufac-turing	Service	Total
1	2	3	4	5	6	7
1.	Making money/profit	Frequency	92	29	20	141
		%	39.3	23.0	22.2	31.3
2.	Want control and freedom	Frequency	5	2	2	9
		%	2.1	1.6	2.2	2.0
3.	Self-reliance	Frequency	49	49	40	138
		%	20.9	38.9	44.4	30.7
4.	To make own decisions	Frequency	9	9	5	23
		%	3.8	7.1	5.6	5.1
5.	Better social status	Frequency	5	6	4	15
		%	2.1	4.8	4.4	3.3
6.	Self achievement	Frequency	65	29	19	113
		%	27.8	23.0	21.1	25.1
7.	Threat of losing job	Frequency	5	0	0	5
		%	2.1	.0	.0	1.1
8.	Family circumstance	Frequency	0	2	0	2
		%	.0	1.6	.0	.4

(Table Contd...)

1	2	3	4	5	6	7
9.	Giving employment to others	Frequency	2	0	0	2
		%	.9	.0	.0	.4
10.	Own business	Frequency	2	0	0	2
		%	.9	.0	.0	.4
	Total	Frequency	234	126	90	450
		%	100.0	100.0	100.0	100.0

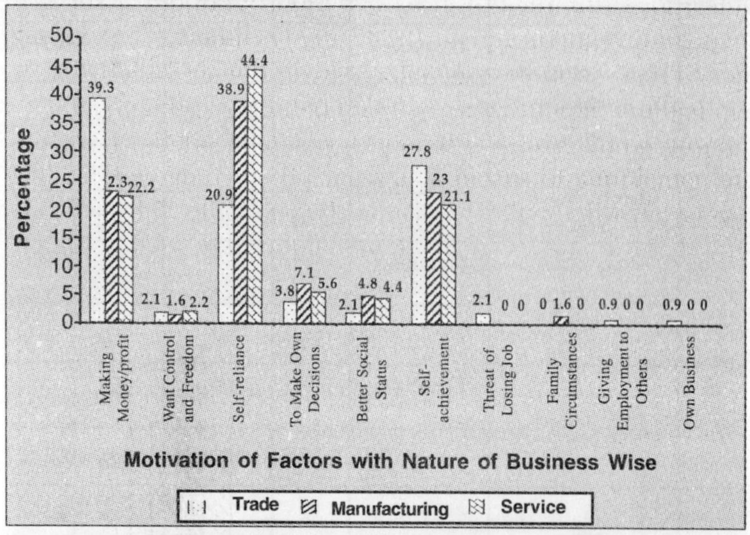

Fig. 4.8: Percentage Distribution of Respondents with Major Motivational Factors for the Business

ISSUES RELATED TO STARTING AND RUNNING THE ENTERPRISE BY WOMEN

The traditional activities segment can be described as consisting mostly of part time business activities carried out at home. They are relying to traditional skills and knowledge that are transferred within the family. Low level risk taking attitude is another factor affecting the women folk's decision to get into business.

Table 4.16

Distribution of Respondents by Reasons to Take up Traditional Business

Sl. No.	Reason		Trade	Manufac-turing	Service	Total
1.	Less risk	Frequency	155	105	75	335
		%	66.2	83.3	83.3	74.4
2.	Forced by circumstances	Frequency	10	2	2	14
		%	4.3	1.6	2.2	3.1
3.	Inherited business	Frequency	35	13	11	59
		%	15.0	10.3	12.2	13.1
4.	Limited Knowledge	Frequency	27	4	1	32
		%	11.5	3.2	1.1	7.1
5.	Any other reason	Frequency	7	2	1	10
		%	3.0	1.6	1.1	2.2
	Total	Frequency	234	126	90	450
		%	100.0	100.0	100.0	100.0

Among the various reasons for having chosen the traditional business by the respondents of the study, it is not surprising to find that nearly 75 per cent of them answered that they do not want to take risk. According to them in the traditional business the risk factor is less.

The reasons attributed are that since the investment level is low combined with low education, it leads to low self confidence, and self- reliance which make the women engage in traditional business. The table 4.16 shows that 13 per cent continued the venture as it was inherited from the past. 7.1 per cent of the respondents acknowledge that their knowledge for modern business is limited and 3 per cent report that they are forced by the circumstance, which is the main reason for traditional take up.

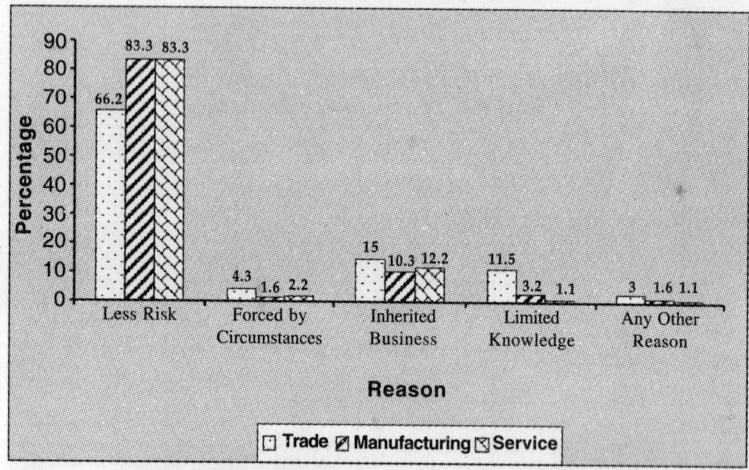

Fig. 4.9: Percentage Distribution of Respondents by Reasons to Take up Traditional Business

Table 4.17

Distribution of Respondents by the Activities Performed at the Time of Start

Sl.No.	List of Activity	Yes	No	Total
1.	Preparation of business plan	12 (2.67)	438 (97.33)	450 (100)
2.	Tested in a Market Place	21 (4.67)	429 (95.33)	450 (100)
3.	Business consultation	82 (18.22)	368 (81.78)	450 (100)
4.	Attended EDP Training	14 (3.11)	436 (96.89)	450 (100)

Fig in () Percentage of respondents.

It is clearly understood that a vast majority of the respondents do not undergo for the initial ground work as in the case of typical business at the time of start. It shows that 97.33 per cent do not spend time for preparation of the plan and 95.33 per cent do not test the sample product in the market. 81.77 per cent do not have functional consultation and 96.88

per cent do not attend EDP training before the start –up. Only less per cent of respondents go for the above mentioned activities at the time of start up.

The disappointing performance of the above activities by women's small business due to the nature of the business, which is highly traditional, that the women choose. These female micro entrepreneurs tend to be minimal, home based, do function with small funds and perform modest sales.

Starting a business is not without obstacles. In fact, the whole process of entrepreneurship seems like overcoming one challenge after the other. All businessmen owners face certain challenges, but women, because of their gender, often have additional challenges and obstacles that their male peers are less likely to encounter. The obstacles might be in the form of economic and psychological aspects. The table 4.18 analyses the major obstacles for starting the business by the respondents.

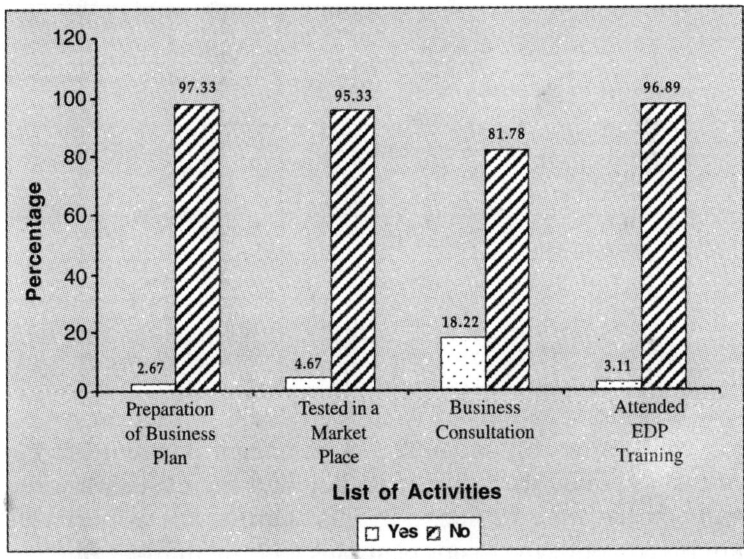

Fig. 4.10: Percentage Distribution of Respondents by the Activities Performed at the time of Start

Table 4.18

Distribution of Respondents by facing Major Obstacles in Starting the Business

Sl. No.	Obstacles in Starting Business		Trade	Manufac-turing	Service	Total
1.	Question of self-confidence	Frequency	1	1	2	4
		%	.4	.8	2.2	.9
2.	Lack of start up finance	Frequency	43	15	9	67
		%	18.4	11.9	10.0	14.9
3.	Lack of information/advice	Frequency	2	0	0	2
		%	.9	.0	.0	.4
4.	Managerial skills	Frequency	41	28	20	89
		%	17.5	22.2	22.2	19.8
5.	Gender discrimination	Frequency	3	5	1	9
		%	1.3	4.0	1.1	2.0
6.	Question of Co-ordinating Family and business life	Frequency	90	66	50	206
		%	38.5	52.4	55.6	45.8
7.	Any other unspecified obstacles	Frequency	51	11	8	3
		%	21.8	8.7	8.9	15.6
8.	No obstacles	Frequency	3	0	0	3
		%	1.3	0	0	.7
	Total	Frequency	234	126	90	450
		%	100.0	100.0	100.0	100.0

It could be observed from the table 4.18 that except 0.7 per cent of the respondents, a close to cent per cent (99.3%) of the respondents report that they had the obstacles when they started their business. In this analysis the respondents are asked about the major obstacles and the number of other problems they faced as well. Among the major obstacles the problem related to coordinating family and business life has been found to be higher. Nearly 46 per cent of the total

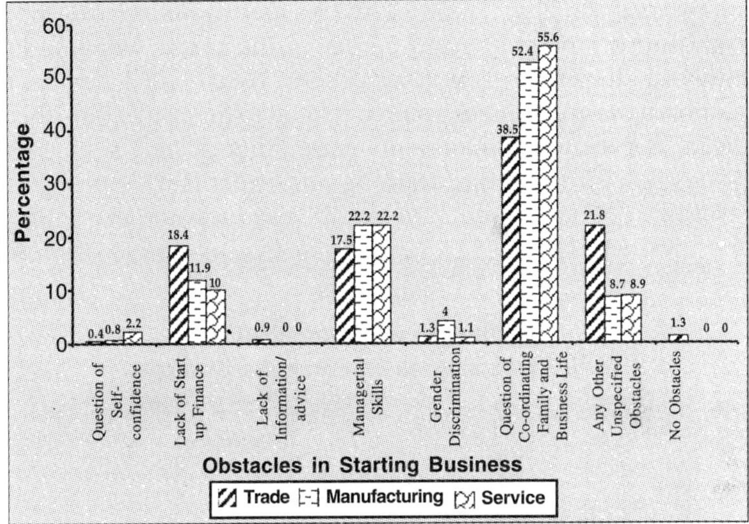

Fig. 4.11: Percentage Distribution of Respondent byFacing Major Obstacles in Starting thc Business

respondents have pointed out this problem. It is followed by the major obstacle viz. Lack of start up finance by 14.9 per cent and the question of lack of management skills 19.8 per cent. The other issues cited by the respondents are the question of self confidence 0.9 per cent, lack of information and advice 0.4 per cent, gender discrimination 2.0 per cent. It is further noted that nearly 16 per cent have unspecified problem in start up.

It is understood that the question of combining career and family is the foremost psychological problem in start up. Similarly raising the finance is the biggest economic problem of micro enterprise but it was not an issue for the start up of business as the SHGs support them in a big way.

Women entrepreneurs have also been questioned about the daily problems they face in running their business. More general questions about the size of their enterprises, their family background and their qualifications are raised in order to complete the picture. It is well known that even though the business activities face several issues particularly related to finance, 66.2 per cent of the respondents report that combining family life and career is the major obstacle in running the business among others. Nearly 22.4 per cent respondents quoted the problem related to finance as the other issue. A very few respondents cited other obstacles such as issues related to getting training and skills (1.8%), problem relating to obtaining materials for the products and marketing the product (4.0%).

Table 4.19

Distribution of Respondent by Major Obstacles in Running the Business

Sl. No.	Obstacles in Running Business		Trade	Manufac-turing	Service	Total
1.	Combining family and business life	Frequency	137	93	68	298
		%	58.5	73.8	75.6	66.2
2.	Liquidity and other financial problems	Frequency	69	18	14	101
		%	29.4	14.2	15.5	22.44
3.	No time for training/ upgrading skills	Frequency	4	2	2	8
		%	1.7	1.6	2.2	1.8
4.	Gaining the acceptance/ respect of people	Frequency	1	0	0	1
		%	.4	.0	.0	.2
5.	Problems related with raw material	Frequency	9	5	4	18
		%	3.8	4.0	4.4	4.0
6.	Problems related to marketing the product	Frequency	9	7	2	18
		%	3.8	5.5	2.2	4.0
7.	No obstacles	Frequency	5	1	0	6
		%	2.1	.8	0	1.3
	Total	Frequency	234	126	90	450
		%	100.0	100.0	100.0	100.0

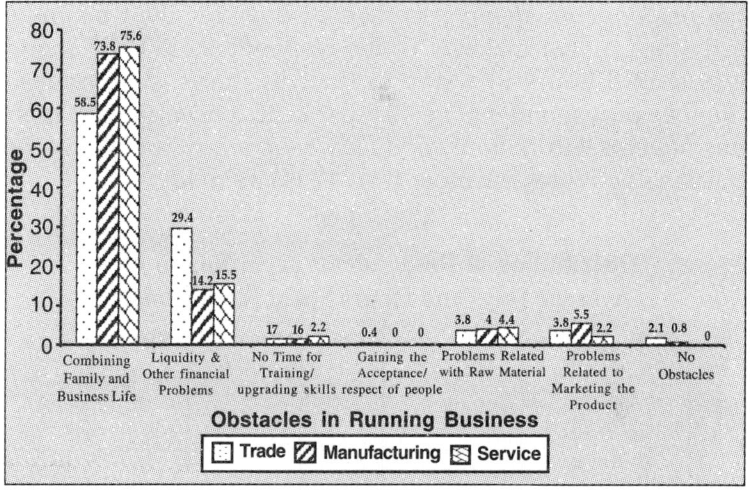

Fig. 4.12: Percentage Distribution of Respondents by Major Obstacles in Running the Business

It can be concluded that the issues of combining career and family life is the major obstacle during start up and running the business by the women entrepreneurs as micro enterprise activities is the next one to the respondents of the study.

Flexibility in behaviour, domestic chores and working hours and adjustment of one with the other are expected to make a greater contribution to the female entrepreneurs. The combination of work and family responsibilities and flexible working hours seem to be an important motive for women to engage in self-employment. Moreover, it has the significant differences among women employed in organisation as the self employment is not subject to many constraints like the former category and they can participate more intensively in either household or business work. The success of an enterprise is always positively correlated with time spent on it by the entrepreneur.

It has been found that a vast majority of respondents (96.9%) average number of working days is from 11 to 20 days. Only 1.3 per cent of the respondents spend their days for business purpose from 21 to 30 days, while 1.1 per cent of the respondents spend less than 10 days for their business activities. A vast majority of the respondents (80.7%) spend less than 8 hours in a day to their business. A minimum number of respondents i.e 10.9 per cent concentrate on their business for 9 to 12 hours and only 8.4 per cent involve in the business activities for more than 12 hours a day.

Table 4.20

Distribution of Respondents according to the Average Days and Hours Spent for Business

Sl. No.	Average Days in Months		Trade	Manufacturing	Service	Total
1.	Less than 10 days	Frequency	7	1	0	8
		%	3	.8	0	1.8
2.	11 to 20 days	Frequency	221	125	90	436
		%	94.4	99.2	100.0	96.88
3.	21 to 30 days	Frequency	6	0	0	6
		%	2.6	.0	.0	1.3
	Total	Frequency	234	126	90	450
		%	100.0	100.0	100.0	100.0
No of Hrs Spend by the respondents						
1.	Less than 8 hours	Frequency	166	112	85	363
		%	70.9	88.9	94.4	80.7
2.	9 to 12 hours	Frequency	40	8	1	49
		%	17.1	6.3	1.1	10.9
3.	More than 12 hours	Frequency	28	6	4	38
		%	12.0	4.8	4.4	8.4
	Total	Frequency	234	126	90	450
		%	100.0	100.0	100.0	100.0

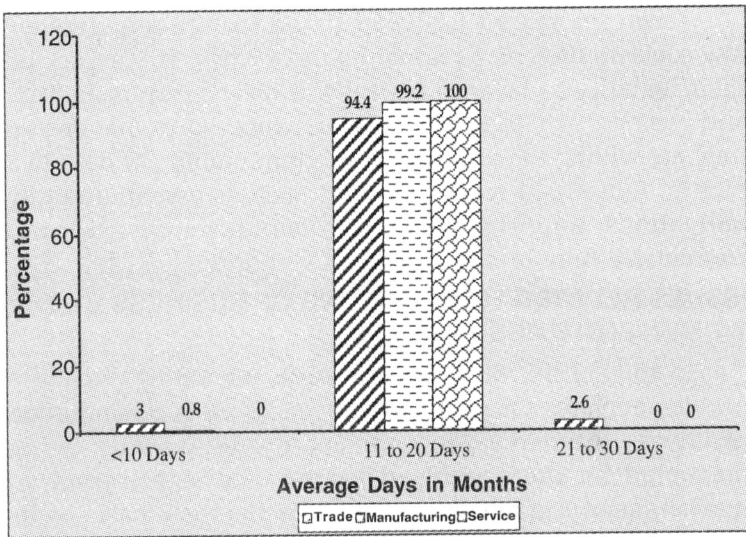

Fig. 4.13: Percentage Distribution of Respondents according to the Average Days Spent for Business

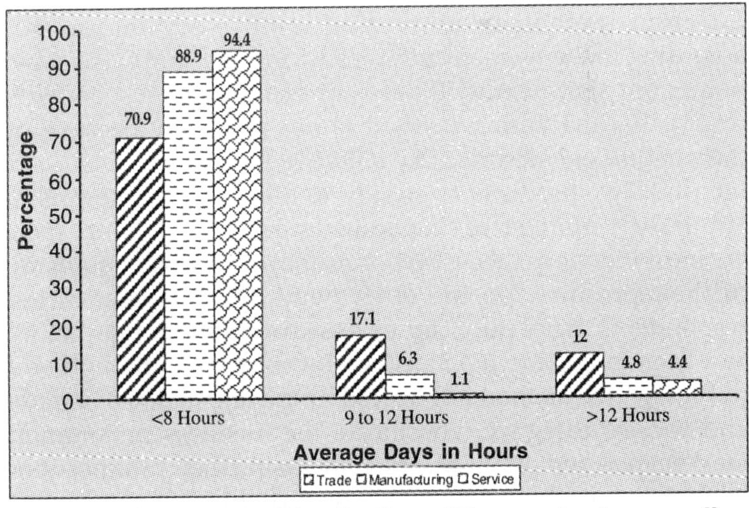

Fig. 4.14: Percentage Distribution of Respondents according to the Average Hours Spent for Business

When the reason has been traced for the respondents' low concentration on days and hours of work, they expressed their inability to balance between domestic responsibilities and business activities. The entrepreneurs report that even if they are willing to work for a maximum number of days in a month, household responsibilities such as essential family obligations, important social ceremonies restrict them to concentrate fully on their business ventures.

ISSUES RELATED TO MARKETING OF BUSINESS BY THE WOMEN ENTREPRENEURS

In spite of the vast domestic work, marketing remains a problematic area for micro enterprises as mass consumption of labour intensive products are predominantly being marketed by the organised sector. The significance of marketing of the micro enterprise is the very basis of its industrial activity. The following tables discuss the practices and methods followed for marketing micro enterprise' products.

Being the size of the venture small and the business turnover low, influencing the customer by way of following different method of marketing is not very important, according to the women entrepreneurs in the study. The table points out that nearly 50 per cent of the total respondents report that marketing method is not necessary because of their nature of enterprise like tailoring shop, small hotels and intermediary products to supply to other small enterprises. Similarly a number of respondents point out that as their business is done in their own house, they do not want publicity of their product. On the other hand 37.4 per cent of the respondents make publicity of their product through family and friends. Next to it 5.5 per cent of them do it through oral publicity. This method is followed by the respondents of trade and service category who locate the business in common market areas and public places. Canvassing their product door to door is found to be 3.8 per cent and only 3.55 per cent of the respondents follow the modern method of marketing like advertisement in local channels and news papers. It can be interpreted that the micro women entrepreneurs in micro level business are yet to realize the importance of marketing and adopt modern marketing techniques for better sales and big profits.

Table 4.21

Distribution of Respondents on the Basis of Methods of Marketing

Sl. No.	Methods of Marketing		Trade	Manufac-turing	Service	Total
1.	Through family and friends	Frequency	80	49	39	168
		%	34.3	38.9	43.3	37.4
2.	From door to door selling	Frequency	9	6	2	17
		%	3.9	4.8	2.2	3.8
3.	Oral publicity	Frequency	18	0	7	25
		%	7.7	0	7.8	5.5
4.	Advertisement in local channels/ Newspapers	Frequency	5	1	0	6
		%	2.1	8.73	.0	3.55
5.	Not necessary to follow any marketing method	Frequency	122	70	42	234
		%	52.13	55.56	46.7	49.7
	Total	Frequency	234	126	90	450
		%	100.0	100.0	100.0	100.0

The mode of sales in traditional business is determined by the nature of the product and the mode differs from one product to another. It has been found that the nature of venture being small, the women entrepreneurs does not follow the modern methods of sale. Since the business is done in their home and at specific places and the customers are mainly from local places, they are well aware of the existence and availability of the product. The table 4.22 shows that nearly 84 per cent of the total respondents' sale of the product is directly to the customers, who come to their shop. Next to it, 9 per cent of the respondents supply to the local shops. Nearly 5 per cent of the women entrepreneurs distribute their goods and services to the shops, which are located in the market area. It further shows that 7 per cent of the respondents in a manufactory field distribute their complementary goods directly to other neighboring business.

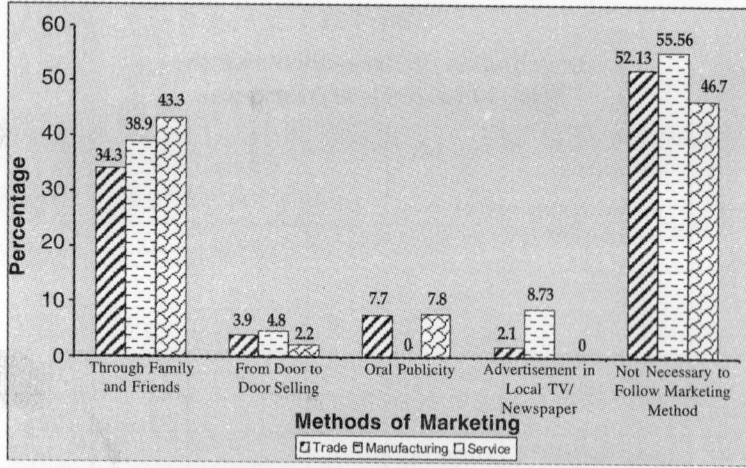

Fig. 4.15: Percentage Distribution of Respondents on the Basis of Methods of Marketing

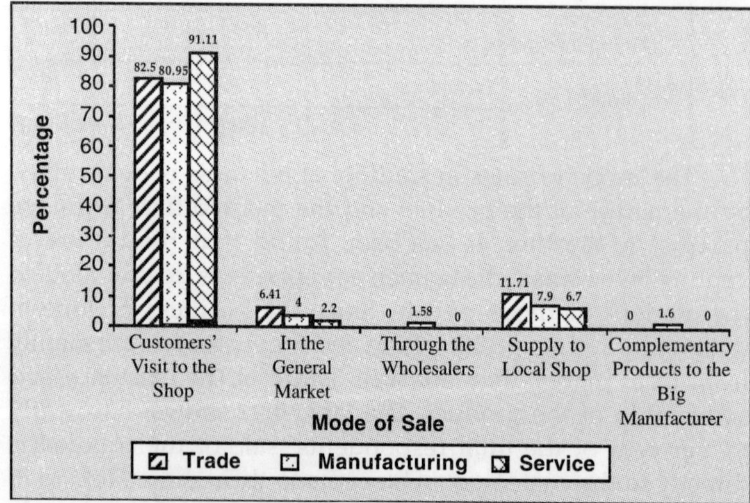

Fig. 4.16: Percentage Distribution of Respondents According to the Mode of Sale of Products and Services

Table 4.22

Distribution of Respondents According to the Mode of Sale of Products and Services

Sl. No.	Mode of Sale		Trade	Manufac-turing	Service	Total
1.	Customers' visit to the shop	Frequency	193	102	82	377
		%	82.5	80.95	91.11	83.77
2.	In the general market	Frequency	15	5	2	22
		%	6.41	4.0	2.2	4.8
3.	Through wholesalers	Frequency	0	2	0	2
		%	0	1.58	.0	.4
4.	Supply to local shops	Frequency	26	10	6	41
		%	11.71	7.9	6.7	9.1
5.	Complementary products to the big manufacturer	Frequency	0	7	0	7
		%	0	1.6	0	1.6
	Total	Frequency	234	126	90	450
		%	100.0	100.0	100.0	100.0

Mode of transport is one of the significant factors determining the sales volume of business as well as the growth of the venture. It is understood that the mode of transport is not a necessary mean for the sales, as number of units have been established mainly in the house of the respondents and in the of stalls of the market. Moreover, the respondents report that their sales volume and revenue generated are not comparable to purchase of high class vehicle such as car/ motorcycle. The table 4.23 shows that a vast majority (85.3%) consider transport as unnecessary for their business. Nearly 7 per cent of the respondents go by walk to the business centre and 3.3 by bicycle. Only 4.4 per cent use motor cycle as mode of transport for business purpose.

Table 4.23

Distribution of Respondents According to the Mode of Transport

Sl. No.	Mode of Transport		Trade	Manufacturing	Service	Total
1.	Two wheeler/car	Frequency	10	6	4	20
		%	4.3	4.8	4.4	4.4
2.	Bicycle	Frequency	12	2	1	15
		%	5.1	1.6	1.1	3.3
3.	By walk	Frequency	20	7	4	31
		%	8.5	5.6	4.4	6.9
4	No need for transport	Frequency	192	111	81	384
		%	82.1	88.1	90.0	85.3
	Total	Frequency	234	126	90	450
		%	100.0	100.0	100.0	100.0

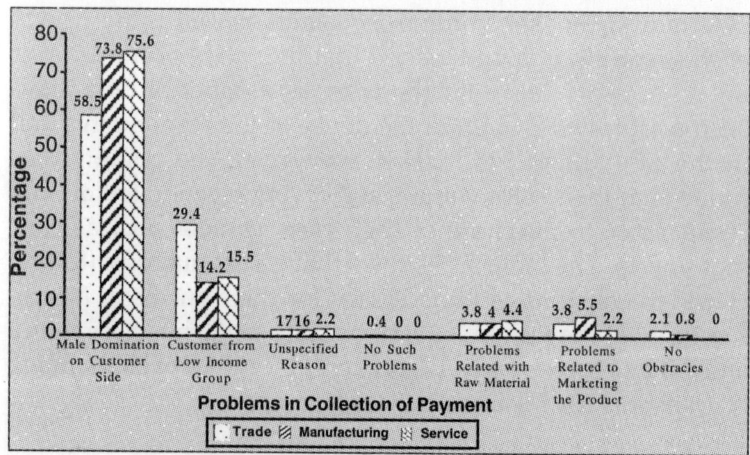

Fig. 4.17: Percentage Distribution of Respondents on the Basis of Major Problem in Collection of Payment

Table 4.24

Distribution of Respondents on the Basis of Major Problem in Collection of Payment

Sl. No.	Problems in Collection of Payment		Trade	Manufac-turing	Service	Total
1.	Male domination on customer side	Frequency	192	114	82	388
		%	82.1	90.5	91.1	86.2
2.	Customer from low income group	Frequency	17	6	6	29
		%	7.3	4.8	6.7	6.4
3.	Unspecified reasons	Frequency	15	3	1	19
		%	6.4	2.4	1.1	4.2
4.	No such problems	Frequency	10	3	1	14
		%	4.3	2.4	1.1	3.1
	Total	Frequency	234	126	90	450
		%	100.0	100.0	100.0	100.0

Collection of payment for the sale of the product of micro enterprises run by the women is found to be a major issue. In this respect the respondents have been asked to choose their main problem even though the entrepreneurs face in reality several issues in marketing the product. A vast majority of respondents (86.2%) reported that their major problem arises from male customers. It is revealed that all categories of business like trade (82.1%) manufacturing (90.5%) and service (96.1%) encounter the same problem. The other reasons are not significant to these women entrepreneur. Only 6.4 per cent of them expressed that the buyers of their products belong to low income group, and 4.2 per cent reported the unspecified problems in collection. It has also been found that only 3 per cent have no such problems referred.

Since the size of the business is at micro level these ventures may have their peak and slump periods. The finding of the study is in contrast with the above opinion. It could be observed that nearly 85 per cent of the respondents report that their business has no peak periods. Only a less percentage of respondents have faced such rare periods. It has been found that 4 per cent of the respondents have reported that the peak time of their business is festive season and 4.9 per cent of respondent quote seasons like winter/summer and only 2.7 per cent report the other reasons.

Table 4.25

Distribution of Respondents by Peak Period of Business

Sl. No.	Peak Period of Business		Trade	Manufac-turing	Service	Total
1.	Functions and Festivals	Frequency	7	7	4	18
		%	3.0	5.6	4.4	4.0
2.	Winter/summer seasons	Frequency	10	7	5	22
		%	4.3	5.6	5.6	4.9
3.	Others	Frequency	7	4	1	12
		%	3.0	3.2	1.1	2.7
4.	No such peak periods	Frequency	210	108	80	398
		%	89.7	85.7	88.9	88.4
	Total	Frequency	234	126	90	450
		%	100.0	100.0	100.0	100.0

Almost all the respondents in all the categories have acknowledged that the demand for their product is facing fluctuations. There are two major reasons cited by the respondents. Maximum of the respondents (99.3%) reported that competitive challenge, which is emanating from the organised sector products, is the major threat for their business, which again is the reason for fluctuation in demand for the product. Only 0.4 per cent respondents of the product from small and micro enterprise have inadequate information about the change in trends as the reason.

ISSUES RELATED WITH LOAN FOR MICRO ENTERPRISES RUN BY WOMEN

In addition to the revolving fund and other financial benefits from government/agencies the women entrepreneurs approach financial institutions for loan to run their business. The approach is made through the respective SHGs. The loan amount is normally obtained either individually or collectively. If the loan is obtained collectively by the group, then amount is equally distributed to the needy members. One of the major constraints faced by them in this aspect is in obtaining the loan eventhough the nature of work requires less capital investment. The problems are in the form of delay in sanctioning the amount, high rate of interest or inadequate amount. There are number of financial institutions lending the amount to the entrepreneurs' viz commercial banks, NBFCs (HDFC, ICICI), Cooperative Banks and Regional Rural Banks (Pandian Gram Bank, Pallavan Gram bank).

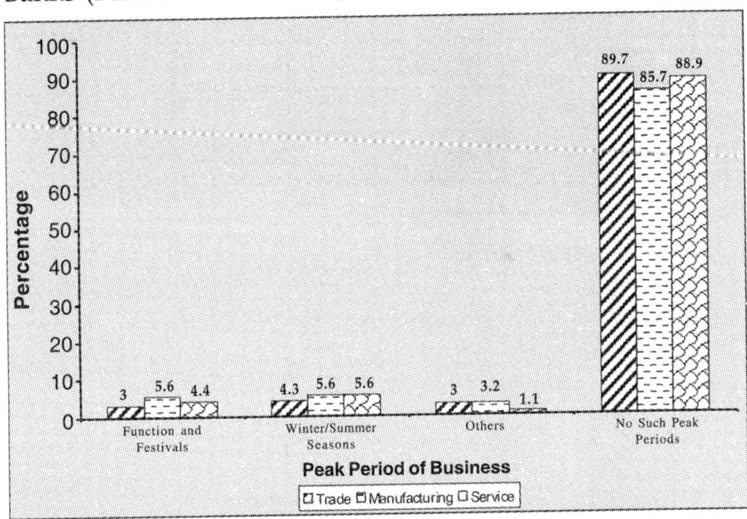

Fig. 4.18: Percentage Distribution of Respondents by Peak Period of Business

It could be observed from table 4.27 that all the respondents of the study had received money by applying for group loans. Nearly fifty per cent of respondents have availed the loan from commercial banks. The co-operative banks (22%) and NBFCs (20.22%) have also played a significant role by extending financial help to the respondents of the study. The contribution of regional rural banks is 11 per cent. However, as discussed above, a vast majority of the respondents reported that they had to meet difficulties in getting the loans. The difficulties are mainly in the form of delay in crediting the amount. The problem is much higher in commercial banks (85%), and Cooperative banks (85.15%), whereas it is less in NBFCs (9.89%) and rural banks (18.36%).

Table 4.26

Distribution of Respondents According to the Fluctuation in Demand for the Product

Sl. No.	Reasons of Fluctuation		Trade	Manufac-turing	Service	Total
1.	Competitive challenges	Frequency	231	126	90	447
		%	98.7	100.0	100.0	99.3
2.	Inadequate information about changing trends	Frequency	2	0	0	2
		%	.9	.0	.0	.4
3.	No such fluctuation	Frequency	1	0	0	1
		%	.4	.0	.0	.2
	Total	Frequency	234	126	90	450
		%	100.0	100.0	100.0	100.0

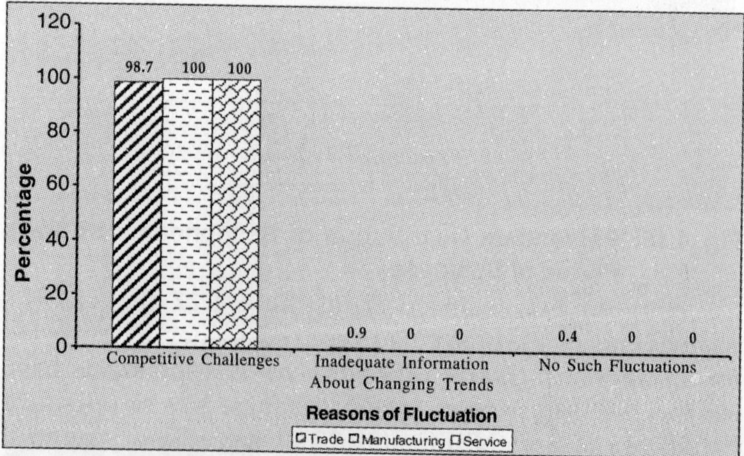

Fig. 4.19: Distribution of Respondents According to the Fluctuation in Demand for the Product

Table 4.27

Distribution of Respondents on the Basis of Sources and Issues in the Loans Obtained

Sl. No.	Source of Loan Obtained		Delay in Obtaining Loan		Total
			Yes	No	
1.	Commercial Banks	Frequency	187	33	220
		%	85	15	48.88
2.	Cooperative Banks	Frequency	9	72	81
		%	9.89	79.12	20.22
3.	Non-banking Financial Institutions	Frequency	86	15	101
		%	85.15	14.85	22.44
4.	Regional Rural Banks	Frequency	9	39	48
		%	18.36	81.25	10.88
	Total	Frequency	291	159	450
		%	64.67	35.33	100

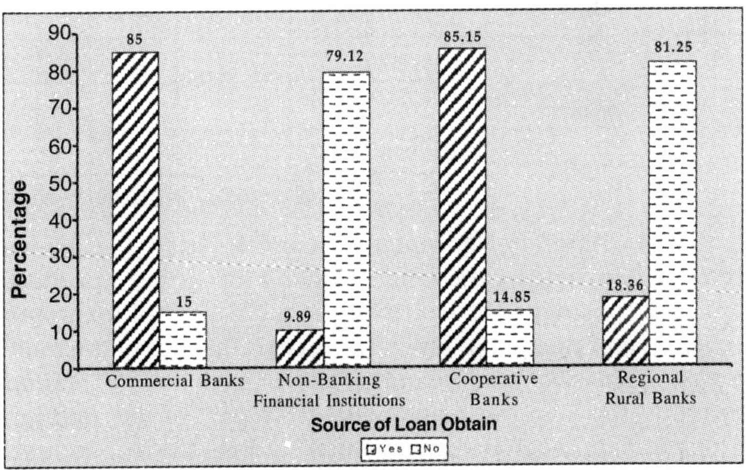

Fig. 4.20: Percentage Distribution of Respondents on the Basis of Sources and Issues in the loans obtained

From the informal discussions with the members and animators (head of the group), commercial banks are the major lending institutions for finance. However, when they are approached for loan, they are restricted by procedural formalities. The banks require production of certificates of not availing loans from the other branches of commercial banks. The formalities are comparatively less in case of rural banks and NBFCs but the rate of interest is high. The amount sanctioned by the cooperative banks is quite inadequate to run the business, according the members of SHGs.

Table 4.28

Distribution of Respondents According to Present Position of Loan

Sl. No.	Present Position		Trade	Manufac-turing	Service	Total
1.	Full amount settled	Frequency	10	11	9	30
		%	4.27	8.73	10.0	6.67
2.	Part of the amount settled	Frequency	211	107	65	383
		%	90.17	84.92	72.22	85.11
3.	Yet to start settling	Frequency	12	8	16	36
		%	5.12	6.34	17.8	8.0
4.	Rate of interest exceeds principal amount	Frequency	01	0	0	1
		%	0.42	-	-	0.22
	Total	Frequency	234	126	90	450
		%	100.0	100.0	100.0	100.0

The women entrepreneurs encounter many problems relating to managing the funds properly for business purpose and this constraint has led to erratic repayment of loans and other related problems. Table 4.28 reveals that out of the total, a vast majority of respondents (85.11%) have already started to repay the loan but could settle only part of the amount. This problem is comparatively higher among the respondents of trade and manufacturing than those in service category. Only 6.67 per cent of the borrowed has settled the entire amount of loan taken from the financial institutions. Moreover 8 per cent of them have yet to start the repayment and one respondent's repayment position is critical as the interest accumulation exceeds the principal amount.

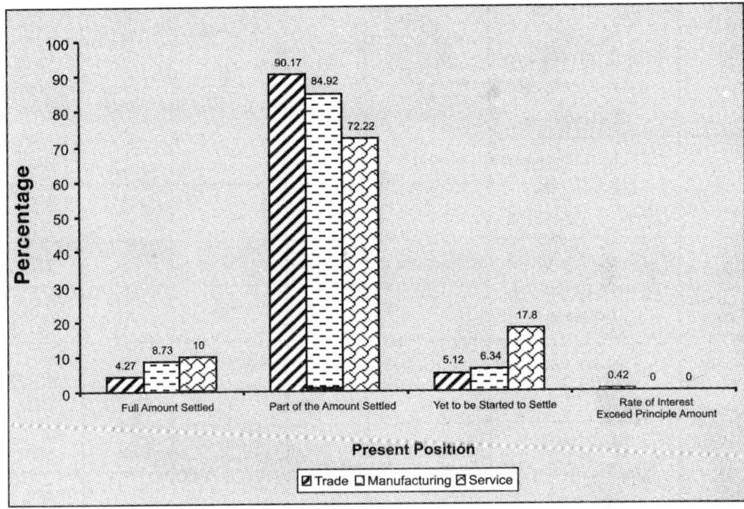

Fig. 4.21: Percentage Distribution of Respondents According to Present Position of Loan

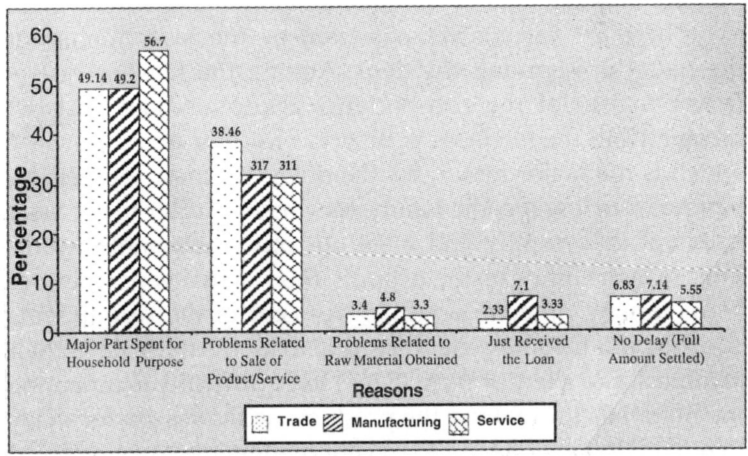

Fig. 4.22: Percentage Distribution of Respondents According to Reasons for Delayed in Repayment of Loan

Table 4.29

Distribution of Respondents According to Reasons for Delayed in Repayment of Loan

Sl. No.	Reasons		Trade	Manufac-turing	Service	Total
1.	Major part spent for household purpose	Frequency	115	62	51	228
		%	49.14	49.20	56.7	50.66
2.	Problems related to sale of product/service	Frequency	90	40	28	158
		%	38.46	31.7	31.1	35.11
3.	Problems related to raw material obtained	Frequency	8	6	3	17
		%	3.4	4.8	3.3	3.8
4.	Just received the loan	Frequency	5	9	3	17
		%	2.33	7.1	3.33	3.8
5.	No delay (full amount settled)	Frequency	16	9	5	30
		%	6.83	7.14	5.55	6.66
	Total	Frequency	234	126	90	450
		%	100.0	100.0	100.0	100.0

There are various reasons cited by the respondents for the delay in repaying the debt. Among the reasons nearly fifty per cent of the respondents acknowledged that the income from the business is diverted for household purpose which is the major reason for the delay. As these women are hailing from low income family, they have to cater to the basic needs of their family and meet out other household needs. This responsibility of them limits their actual repayment of loan. Among other reasons, 35 per cent of the respondents cite the poor income generation due to ineffective sale of their products, and a few of them (3.8%) have difficulty in obtaining the materials for making the products as the reason for delay to repay. However nearly 4 per cent of them have just received the amount from the financial institutions and they have yet to start to repay. The other 6.66 per cent of respondents do not come into the analysis as they have already defrayed their debts.

ISSUES RELATED TO SKILL ACQUISITION FOR RUNNING THE BUSINESS

The traditional segment of the business community normally has low level of formal education. These women generally receive their business skills and acumen from the traditional skills of the family or through some form of informal training. This enhances their practicable entrepreneurial skills to start up a business.

Table 4.30

Distribution of Respondents on the Basis of Sources of Previous Skill Acquisition

Sl. No.	Sources		Trade	Manufacturing	Service	Total
1.	Training course	Frequency	84	67	49	200
		%	35.9	53.2	54.4	44.4
2.	Practical experience	Frequency	111	38	26	175
		%	47.4	30.2	28.9	38.9
3.	From Family members	Frequency	22	13	9	44
		%	9.4	10.3	10.0	9.8
4.	Inborn skill	Frequency	7	5	4	16
		%	3.0	4.0	4.4	3.6
5.	Previous work experience	Frequency	5	2	2	9
		%	2.1	1.6	2.2	2.0
6.	Institutional training from School or College	Frequency	5	1	0	6
		%	2.1	.8	.0	1.3
	Total	Frequency	234	126	90	450
		%	100.0	100.0	100.0	100.0

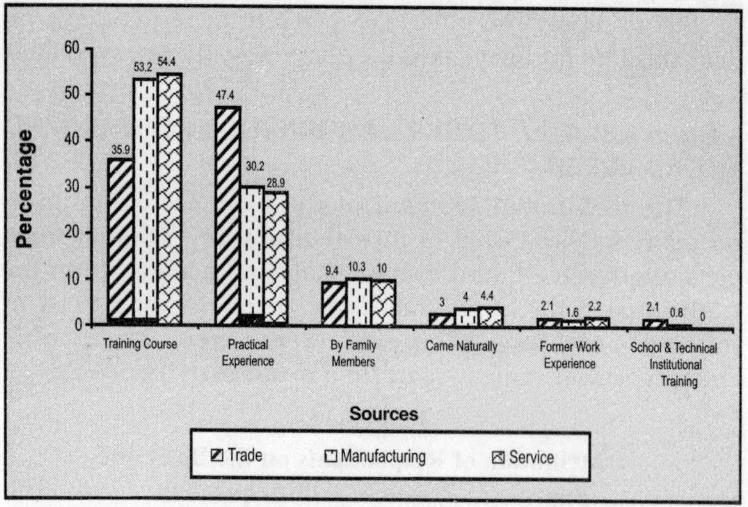

Fig. 4.23: Percentage Distribution of Respondent on the Basis of Sources of Previous Skill Acquisition

The women entrepreneurs, who are members of women SHGs, are given training (normally 4 days) at the time of starting their business. According to the respondents this training is formal and it has helped them a little. The table 4.30 reveals that although all the members have received a formal training from SHGs only 44 per cent have acknowledged that the concerned training is only a small step as the source of skill acquisition. The remaining respondents cited different sources as the main driving force for their skill acquisition. Out of them, nearly 40 have per cent have gained knowledge from actual business practices. 9.8 per cent have obtained skills from the family members. Similar proportion of them has acquired skills for business through previous work experience. It is quite interesting to note that 3.6 per cent have not cited any source but they have the knowledge and skill of their work by birth.

ISSUES RELATED TO BALANCING HOUSEHOLD CHORES AND BUSINESS WORK

The success of a business depends on the support of the family members extended to women entrepreneurs in the business process and management. The interest of the family members is the determining factor in motivating the business aspiration of the womenfolk. Family support helps a lot of self-employed women in running the business effectively. The following tables examine the issues of women entrepreneurs on balancing household chores and business responsibilities.

Table 4.31

Distribution of Respondents on the Basis of Role of Family Members in Business

Sl. No.	Role of Family Members		Trade	Manufac-turing	Service	Total
1.	Partners	Frequency	6	4	4	14
		%	2.6	3.2	4.4	3.1
2.	Well wishers	Frequency	119	67	40	226
		%	50.9	53.2	44.4	50.2
3.	Working partners	Frequency	60	10	6	71
		%	25.64	7.9	6.7	16.8
4.	No such above roles	Frequency	49	45	40	134
		%	20.9	35.7	44.	29.8
	Total	Frequency	234	126	90	450
		%	100	100	100	100

It has been found from the above table that 50 per cent of the respondent's family members have been the well wishers and they encourageb them to do the business but they do not actively engage themselves in business activities. Similarly 3.1 per cent have partners but not engaged in day to day business activities. According to the respondents the members in the concerned family have limited their role only to dealing finance and accounts. It is also stated that 17 per cent of the respondents' family members are working partners in the business wherein their spouses or mother-in-low or other family members join and involve themselves in the business activities of the respondents, like procuring materials, sales activities etc. On the contrary, nearly 30 per cent of the study respondents have not received any support from their family members and they have to meet the challenge on their own.

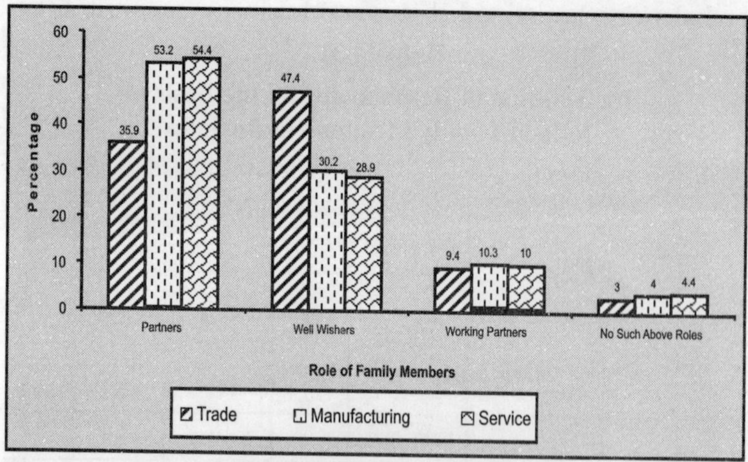

Fig. 4.24: Percentage Distribution of Respondents on the Basis of Role of Family Members in Business

Family support at the entry stage is, however, essential and crucial for entrepreneurial success of women entrepreneurs. There is a major positive response from the families of women entrepreneurs in showing the attitudinal change after the success /running the business. From the outcome of informal discussions with these women respondents, the researcher has come to know that the family members, particularly the husband, was an opponent at the time of start. After the business was well established he has an inclination to support. The table 4.32 shows that nearly 64 per cent of the husbands of these entrepreneurs have turned to become supporters, while 14.4 per cent have remained as opponents. It also shows that nearly 20 per cent of the husbands were not opponents at the time of start. Similar to the above the other groups of opponents have become supporters (70%,

65.8% and 67.8%). It is further understood from the table that the in-laws and parents stand higher in percentage as opponents and surprisingly the husbands were comparatively lower than others. The analysis is not applicable to the few respondents as the respective opponents are not residing with them.

Table 4.32

Attitudinal Change of the Opponents after the Establishment of the Business

Sl. No.	Opponents		Yes	No	No Opponents at the Time of Start	Not Applicable	Total
1.	Husband	Frequency	286	65	88	11	450
		%	63.6	14.4	19.6	2.4	100
2.	Relatives/ friends	Frequency	301	89	60	0	450
		%	66.9	19.8	13.3	0	100
3.	Parents	Frequency	296	112	16	26	450
		%	65.8	24.9	3.6	5.7	100
4.	In laws	Frequency	304	101	16	29	450
		%	67.6	22.4	3.6	6.4	100

Family and spouse support is important for an analysis of women entrepreneurship. Along with the family members, the spouse of the women can help in many ways in the starting as well as running the businesses. The table (4.33) analyses the support and performance of business activities of the women entrepreneurs in the study. It reveals that among the family members the spouse support to the respondents is much appreciable. The support of other family members is found to be limited in major part of the business activities.

Table 4.33

Performance of Business Activities by Family Members in the Business

Sl. No.	Activities		Myself	Husband	Parent/other Family Members	All my Family Members	My Employee Business	Not done in my	Total
1	2		3	4	5	6	7	8	9
1.	Purchasing material	f	184	255	2	2	4	3	450
		%	40.9	56.7	.4	.4	.9	.7	100
2.	Sales	f	330	70	1	37	8	4	450
		%	73.3	15.6	.2	8.1	1.8	.9	100
3.	Marketing of products	f	370	73	3	2	2	–	450
		%	82.2	16.2	.7	.4	.4	–	100
4.	Administration	f	370	72	3	2	0	3	450
		%	82.2	16.0				.7	100
5.	Estimating selling price	f	345	101	–	–	–	1	450
		%	76.7	22.4	–	–	–	.2	100
6.	Estimating business revenue	f	198	246	2	–	1	3	450
		%	44.0	54.7	.4	–	.2	.7	100

(Table Contd…)

1	2		3	4	5	6	7	8	9
7.	File Maintenance	f	258	182	6	3	–	1	450
		%	57.3	40.4	1.3	.7	–	.2	100
8.	Banking activities	f	272	139	34	4	–	1	450
		%	60.4	30.9		.9		.2	100
9.	General/Legal issues	f	129	126	163	29	2	1	450
		%	28.7	28.0	36.2	6.4	.4	.2	100
10.	Planning	f	137	51	142	117	–	1	450
		%	30.4		31.1	26.0	–	.2	100
11.	Others works	f	127	125	163	30	3	2	450
		%	28.2	27.8	36.2	6.7	.7	.4	100

F: Frequency

Among the eleven parameters of business performance activities, the husband's support is found to be highly strong in the area of purchasing materials (56.7%), for the business. The respondents have cited that since they are females and take care of household chores, they are not able to move to long distance, and hence they resort to the help of their husbands. The other major activity of the husband is the estimation of business revenue, (54.7%) file maintenance (40.7%), and banking activities (30.9%). In certain aspects such as dealing the legal issues of the enterprise and planning the business, the support of the family members is found to be considerable. It further shows that majority of the women entrepreneurs focus their mind on the area of sale of products (73.3%), marketing area of business (82.2%), administration (82.2%), and estimating the cost and fixing the selling price (76.7%). It can be interpreted that the spouse of the respondents extends their help the growth of the enterprise in all ways possible.

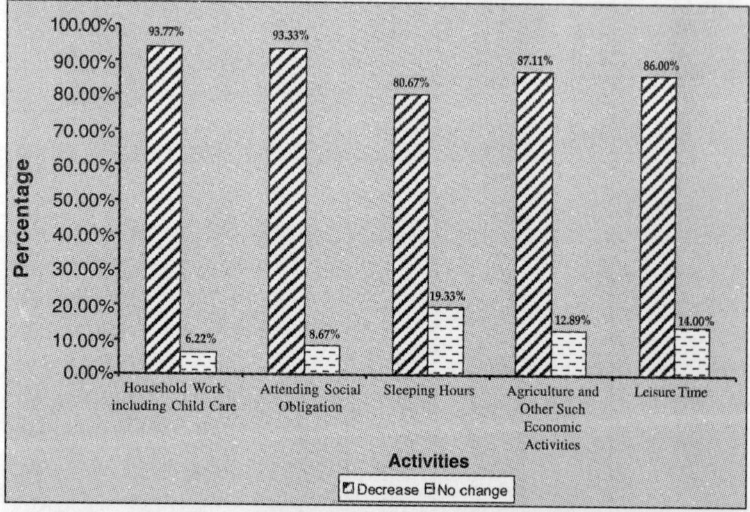

Fig. 4.25: Percentage Distribution of Respondents on Basis of Impact of Business Activities and Commitments on Household Chores

Table 4.34

Distribution of Respondents on the basis of Impact of Business Activities and Commitments on Household Chores

Sl. No.	Activities	Nature of Changes			
		Decreased	No Change	Increased	Total
1.	House hold work including Child care	422	28	Nil	450
		93.77%	6.22%		100%
2.	Attending Social obligations	411	39	Nil	450
		93.33%	8.67%		100%
3.	Sleeping hours	363	87	Nil	450
		80.67%	19.33%		100%
4.	Agriculture and other such economic activities	392	58	Nil	450
		87.11%	12.89%		100%
5.	Leisure time	387	63	Nil	450
		86.0%	14.0%		100%

It is not surprising to note that the women with greater responsibilities in business activities have been greatly diverted from the day to day household activities. An issue often cited as problematic one for women business owners is the task of balancing the responsibilities associated with their business commitments and their of household chores. As it is expected, a vast majority of the respondents in all the categories, viz Trade, Manufacturing & Service have reported that their activities towards household chores, have experienced negative impact. The table 4.34 reveals that 93.77 per cent have cited that their time spent for household work including child care has decreased. Similarly 93.33 per cent acknowledged that their activities in attending social ceremonies have also decreased. The impact of high concentration of women in business activities has decreased their sleeping hours (80.67%) agriculture and other economic activities (87.11%) and the leisure time (86.%) also. Only a few percentages of them cited their involvement in business has never decreased the time in spending for household works and activities.

In the discussions with the entrepreneurs many have reported that they have to work for long hours and carry the weight of responsibility of the business particularly the women in business than those at home. They return home overcome by fatigue and tiredness and they have to engage themselves in the household chores at once. Hence they have difficulty in relaxing at home. Due to their commitment and greater responsibilities of business they have to make personal sacrifices for the sake of success in business.

SUCCESS IN BUSINESS AND FUTURE ASPIRATIONS OF ENTREPRENEURS

Success in the female entrepreneurial context is based on the entrepreneurs' individual experiences. More often success is accompanied by other outcome measures, such as growth in sales, employment, profitability, and productivity.

Table 4.35

Distribution of Respondents on the Basis of the Entrepreneurs Success Level

Sl. No.	Level of Success		Trade	Manufac-turing	Service	Total
1.	Not so successful	Frequency	3	0	0	3
		%	1.3	.0	.0	.7
2.	Success to some extent	Frequency	58	79	63	200
		%	24.8	62.7	70.0	44.4
3.	Success up to entrepreneur's expectation	Frequency	142	34	26	202
		%	60.7	27.0	28.9	44.9
4.	Success beyond entrepreneur's expectation	Frequency	30	11	0	41
		%	12.8	8.7	.0	9.1
5.	Loss beyond entrepreneur's expectation	Frequency	1	2	1	4
		%	.4	1.6	1.1	.9
	Total	Frequency	234	126	90	450
		%	100.0	100.0	100.0	100.0

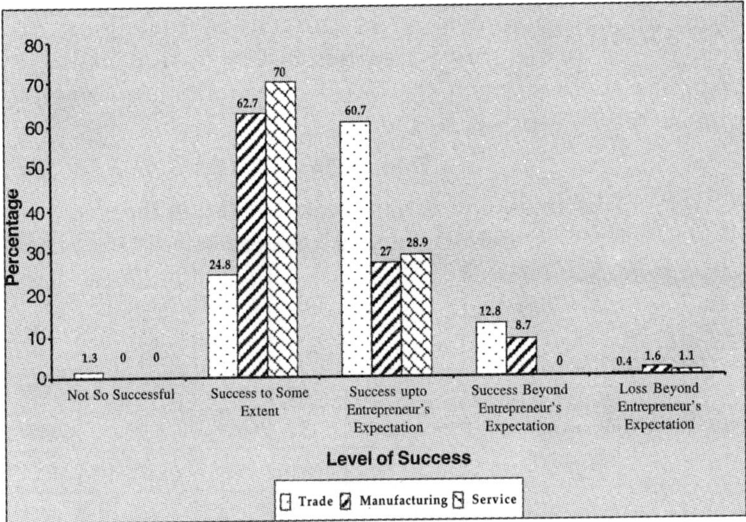

Fig. 4.26: Percentage Distribution of Respondents on the Basis of the entrepreneurs Success Level

The success level of the women entrepreneurs in the study was also assessed. Among the five level factors, it is quite surprising to note that only less per cent of respondents have revealed negative expression about their business. Among them 0.7 per cent of the respondents have reported that their business was not successful, yet they wish to continue their business further. On the contrary 0.9 per cent of the total respondents have the intention to close their business. It could be inferred and understood that most of the women entrepreneurs in the study run the business with the desirable level of success.

The table 4.35 shows that 44.4 per cent of the total respondents have been running the business with the certain level of success and an equal proportion of the total respondents (44.9%) have reported that their business yields success up to their expectation. The above said level of success has been found much higher in respect of trade business (60.7%). Only 9 per cent of the total respondents have reported that the success rate has been beyond their expectation level.

From the above analysis it is understood that the micro enterprises in the study area has not been flourishing to complete success, but it reaches the desirable level so as to pursue the enterprises further.

Table 4.36

Distribution of Respondents by Rating the Performance in Business

Sl. No.	Performance Areas of Rating		Good	Poor	Excellent	Total
1.	Work life balance	Frequency	152	284	14	450
		%	33.8	63.1	3.1	100
2.	Financial benefits	Frequency	351	89	10	450
		%	78.0	19.8	2.2	100
3.	Communications	Frequency	387	61	2	450
		%	86.0	13.6	0.4	100
4.	Career/personal development	Frequency	363	75	12	450
		%	80.7	16.7	2.7	100
5.	Ability to take initiatives	Frequency	301	143	6	450
		%	66.9	31.8	1.3	100
6.	Social upliftment	Frequency	311	135	4	450
		%	69.1	30.0	.9	100

Since the small business and micro enterprise sector under the purview of women's Self Help Groups have been the tools for enhancing the empowerment of women, the performance of this venture on different parameters has been given rating such as work life balance, finance, communications, career development, ability to take initiative and social upliftment. The aspect of work life balance has been rated well by 34 per cent of women respondents. The same was rated poor by nearly 63 per cent and is marked excellent by only 3.1 per cent. Many of the women entrepreneurs have reported that the family obligation bars them from becoming successful entrepreneurs. Having primary responsibilities for children, elder dependent family members, they have to devote their

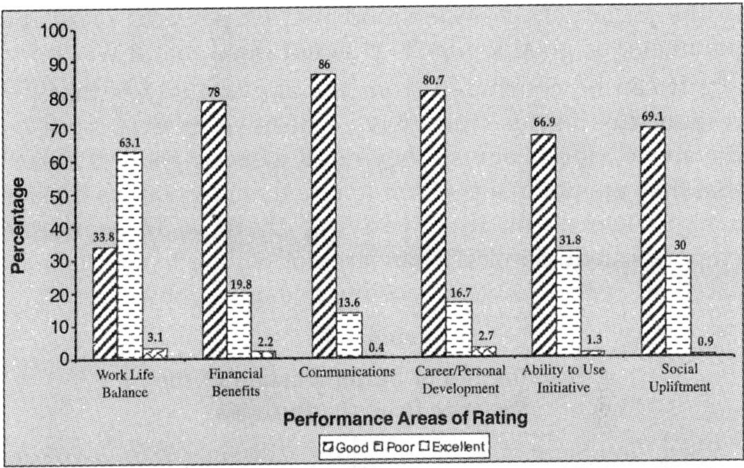

Fig. 4.27: Percentage Distribution of Respondents by Rating the Performance in Business

time to house chores and make a fine balance between domestic and business responsibilities. It is really appreciable that 78 per cent of the respondents have rated good in the aspect of financial benefits, whilst nearly 20 per cent only have rated it as poor. Many respondents have reported in this particular aspect that even though the business does not make them sound financially it adds economic sustenance of life as they have some opportunity to make money. The other aspect, as development of communication skill shows that a vast majority of them (86%) rate it as good, 13.6 rate it as poor and only 0.4 per cent rate as excellent. Due to their involvement in small business, it has continued to career/ personnel development as good by nearly 81 per cent. Almost 17 per cent of the respondents felt career development is poor and only 2.7 per cent rate it as excellent. Nearly 70 per cent of the respondents have obtained the ability to take their initiatives as good whilst 32 per cent have rated it as negative and 1.3 per cent has chosen it as excellent. One of the important abilities the respondents have acquired due to the involvement of micro enterprise is social upliftment, as it creates a good network of familiarity and opportunities among the women in the society. It is understood that 69 per cent rated the parameter as good whilst 30 per cent rated that it was poor.

It can be concluded from the above analysis that the respondents in this study have a positive modest mind on the above aspects and so they rated them as good. It means that they are not in a position to rate them as poor as it plays a significant role in improving their socio-economic empowerment. Similarly they are not willing to cite them as excellent as the business encounters many problems.

Table 4.37

Distribution of Major Portion of the Revenue from the Business

Sl. No.	Investment in Business		Trade	Manufac-turing	Service	Total
1.	Re-Investment in business	Frequency	76	24	12	112
		%	32.6	19.0	13.3	24.9
2.	Repaying loans	Frequency	113	94	71	278
		%	48.5	74.6	78.9	61.9
3.	Use of funds for family purpose	Frequency	30	4	4	38
		%	12.9	3.2	4.4	8.5
4.	Savings	Frequency	14	4	3	21
		%	6.0	3.2	3.3	4.7
	Total	Frequency	233	126	90	449
		%	100.0	100.0	100.0	100.0

It could be observed from the Table 4.37 that two-fifth of the respondents distribute their revenue arising from their business to repay the loan amount, either the interest or the principal amount. It is disappointing to observe that only 25 per cent of them invest the revenue and plough them back in the same business for further expansion. Moreover 8.5 per cent of the women entrepreneurs distribute their major revenue to their family obligations and only 4.7 per cent of the respondents attempt to save their revenue. Many report that they are not able to divert some part of their business earnings for household purposes as their business is so new that the earning goes for either re-investment or repayment of loans. However they have full confidence that in future they will be able to provide adequate resources for household purposes.

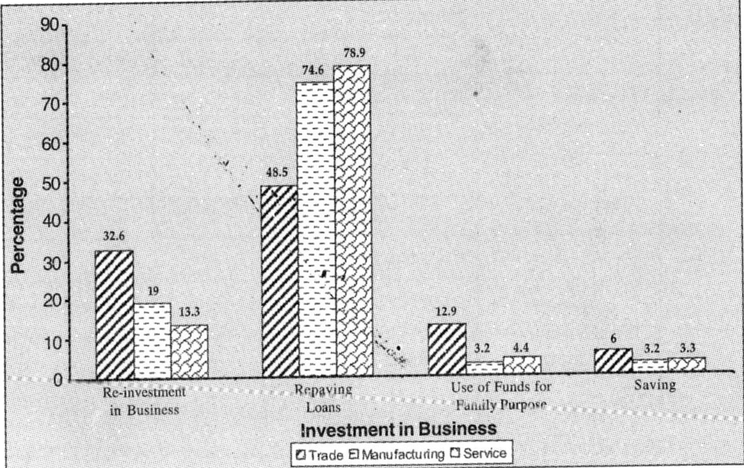

Fig. 4.28: Percentage Distribution of Major Portion of the Revenue from the Business

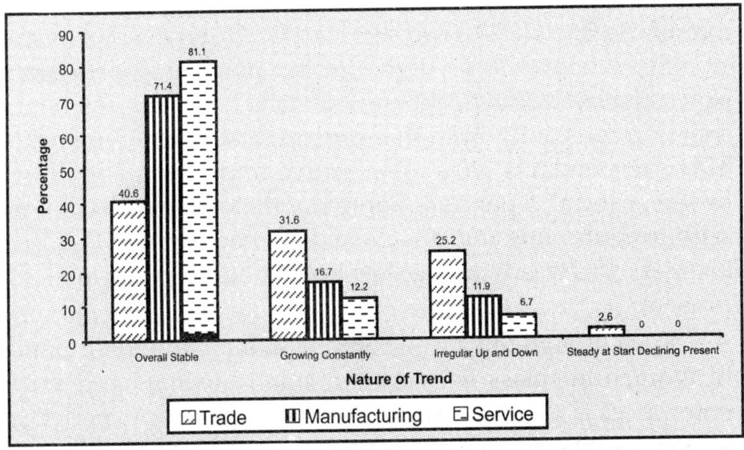

Fig. 4.29: Percentage Distribution of Respondent on the Basis of their Opinion about the Growth Trend Since Startup

Table 4.38

Distribution of Respondents on the Basis of their Opinion about the Growth Trend Since Startup

Sl. No.	Nature of Trend		Trade	Manufacturing	Service	Total
1.	Stable overall	Frequency	95	90	73	258
		%	40.6	71.4	81.1	57.3
2.	Growing constantly	Frequency	74	21	11	106
		%	31.6	16.7	12.2	23.6
3.	Irregular with ups and downs	Frequency	59	15	6	80
		%	25.2	11.9	6.7	17.8
4.	Steady at start but declining at present	Frequency	6	0	0	6
		%	2.6	.0	.0	1.3
	Total	Frequency	234	126	90	450
		%	100.0	100.0	100.0	100.0

The growth trend of the business since the start up reveals that though the business has small up and down the condition and growth of business since startup remain stable as reported by 57.3 per cent of respondents. The respondents in manufacturing (71.4%) and service, (81.1%) report that overall stability is found to be high. Similar positive impression is expressed by 23.6 per cent and they cite that their business is growing constantly from the start up. The remaining portion of the respondents have the negative impression about their business and 17.8 per cent report that their business is moving with irregular ups and downs and 1.3 per cent cite that their business was steady at the start but is poor in performance at present.

Even though female entrepreneurship and the formation of women business networks in small business and micro enterprises is steadily rising, many of them have experienced a considerable amount of dissatisfaction with the performance of business. This is widely due to the fact that many challenges exist for them to overcome. The problem is due to both economic factors such as issues related to finance, marketing etc., and non --economic factors viz., work –family conflict, stress.

Table 4.39

Distribution of Respondents According to their Dissatisfaction in Business for Economic Reasons

Sl. No.	Reason for Dissatisfaction	.	Trade	Manufac-turing	Service	Total
1.	Lack of finance and equipment	Frequency	121	45	21	187
		%	51.7	35.71	42.0	41.5
2.	Too little income generation	Frequency	59	57	47	163
		%	25.2	45.2	52.2	36.2
3.	Problem related marketing	Frequency	30	20	20	70
		%	12.8	15.87	22.2%	15.55
4.	Other economic reasons	Frequency	22	4	2	28
		%	9.4	3.17	2.22	6.22
5.	Highly satisfied	Frequency	2	0	0	2
		%	0.8	0	0	0.4
	Total	Frequency	234	126	90	450
		%	100.0	100.0	100.0	100.0

Almost all the respondents have the feeling of dissatisfaction over the functions of micro enterprises even if they provide a means of livelihood for many women. It does not mean that they have been doing the business in desperation. The level of dissatisfaction emerges due to some kind of negative economic and non-economic forces. An attempt is made to find out the most important factor for the dissatisfaction of the women entrepreneur both for economic and non- economic reasons.

The table 4.39 shows that lack of finance and equipment has been the major factor - the economic reason for dissatisfaction. Next 32. 2 per cent have cited that too little income generation is the cause of dissatisfaction. Marketing has been another major issue for the reason for dissatisfaction as reported by 15.5 per cent whilst 6.22 per cent cite other economic reasons for the dissatisfaction of the women entrepreneurs.

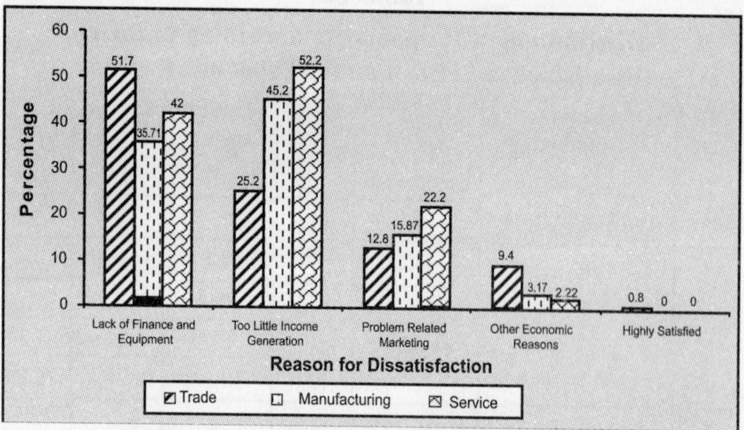

Fig. 4.30: Percentage Distribution of Respondents According to their Dissatisfaction in Business for Economic Reasons

It could be further understood that even though the respondents achieve desirable level of success in the operation of business, they feel somewhat dissatisfied in their business. The reasons are found different from one entrepreneur to another entrepreneur. Similarly all the respondents have shown the symptom of dissatisfaction, whilst the level is different.

Among the non economic reasons for the dissatisfaction in the business there are four major reasons specified. The above table 4.40 shows that 34 per cent of the total respondents undergo stress in their business, among which the respondents' dissatisfaction in trade category (44.0%) is higher than the other categories. Equal proportion of respondents have the feeling that they are inadequate motivational factors for running the business. It is surprising that only 24.2 per cent of the respondents have expressed their dissatisfaction due to issues relating to work life imbalance. The remaining 8 per cent of the respondents report that dissatisfaction is due to inadequate time to attend social obligations.

Table 4.40

Distribution of Respondents According to Non-economic Reasons for Dissatisfaction

Sl. No.	Reasons		Trade	Manufac-turing	Service	Total
1.	Stress is higher in the business	Frequency	103	35	16	154
		%	44.0	27.8	17.8	34.2
2.	Work life imbalance	Frequency	38	37	34	109
		%	16.2	29.4	37.8	24.2
3.	Inadequate motivational factors	Frequency	77	44	30	151
		%	32.9	34.9	33.3	33.6
4.	Constraints in attending social obligations	Frequency	16	10	10	36
		%	6.8	7.9	11.1	8.0
	Total	Frequency	234	126	90	450
		%	100.0	100.0	100.0	100.0

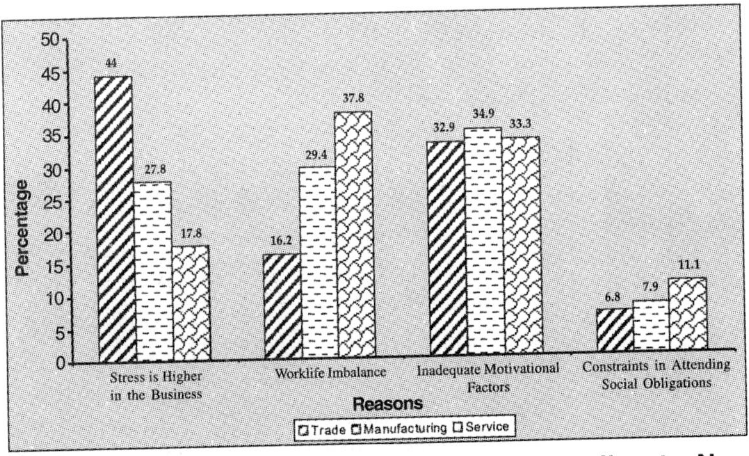

Fig. 4.31 Distribution of Respondents According to Non Economic Reasons for Dissatisfaction

Table 4.41
Distribution of Respondents by the Future Plan of the Entrepreneurship

Sl. No.	Future Plan		Trade	Manufac-turing	Service	Total
1.	To continue in the business	Frequency	157	100	80	337
		%	67.09	79.4	88.9	74.88
2.	To expand the business	Frequency	23	21	10	54
		%	9.82	16.7	11.1	12.0
3.	To start new enterprise too	Frequency	14	1	0	15
		%	5.98	.8	.0	3.33
4.	No decision taken yet	Frequency	40	4	0	44
		%	17.1	3.2	.0	9.8
	Total	Frequency	234	126	90	450
		%	100.0	100.0	100.0	100.0

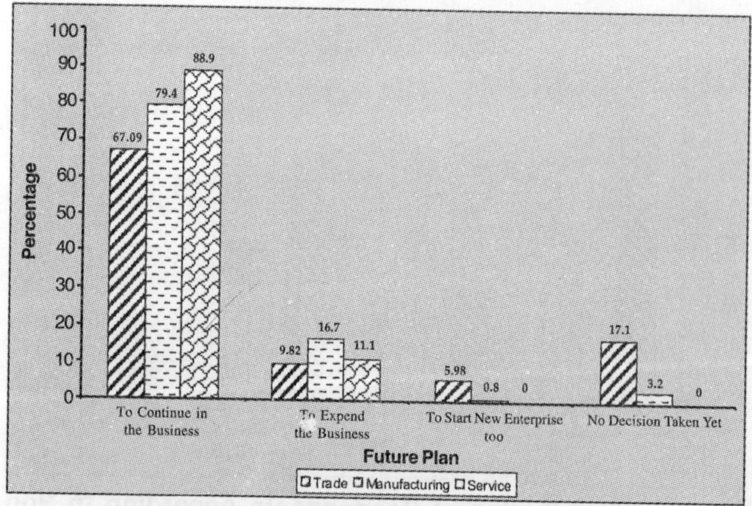

Fig. 4.32: Percentage Distribution of Respondents by the Future Plan of the Entrepreneurship

In spite of the several issues faced by the women entrepreneurs, as per this study, related to economic and non economic aspects, their attitude towards holding on the business is quite optimistic; two-third of them want to continue their present business but they have no intention to expand it. Among them, the respondents in service who have (89%) desire to hold on are much higher. It further shows that 12 per cent have the intention to expand the present business, whilst 3.33 per cent of the total respondents have the idea to start a new enterprise in addition to the present one. In contrast 9.8 per cent of the entrepreneurs have no future plan, as these entrepreneurs are on great losses; they have no idea to wind up the present one nor continues the same. It can be concluded that the analysis with regard to the future plan of the entrepreneurs is found to be optimistic in the context of planning the future of their enterprise.

Table 4.42

Distribution of Respondents on the Basis of Reasons for not Expanding their Business

Sl. No.	Reasons for not Expanding Business		Trade	Manufacturing	Service	Total
1.	Inadequate income	Frequency	155	93	80	328
		%	62.23	73.805	88.88	72.89
2.	Difficult due to domestic responsibilities	Frequency	53	11	0	64
		%	22.64	8.7	.0	14.22
3.	Present one is enough	Frequency	3	1	0	4
		%	1.3	.8	.0	.9
4.	Interested in expanding business	Frequency	23	21	10	54
		%	9.82	16.60	11.11	12.0
	Total	Frequency	234	126	90	450
		%	100.0	100.0	100.0	100.0

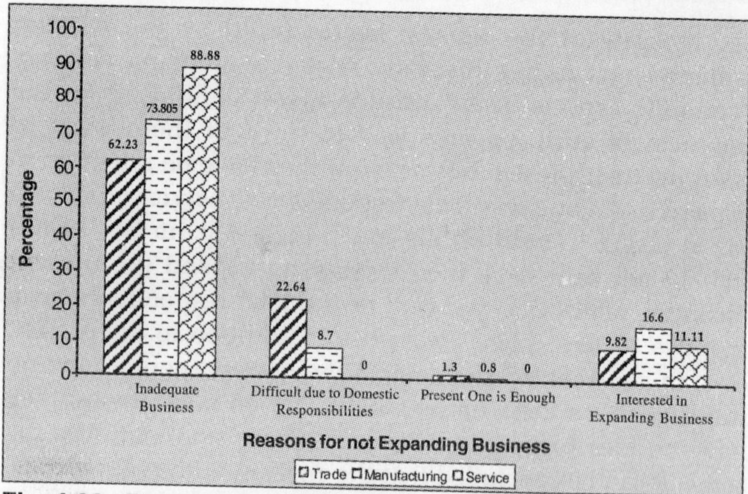

Fig. 4.33: Percentage Distribution of Respondents on the Basis of Reasons for not Expanding their Business

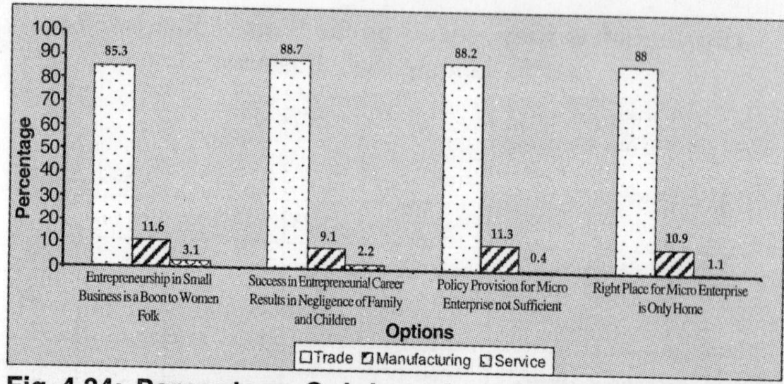

Fig. 4.34: Percentage Opinion of respondents about the Involvement of Women in Small and Micro Enterprises

It is really disappointing that except 12 per cent of the total women entrepreneurs in the study, the remaining (88%) are not willing or unable to go on for further expansion of business. Certain reasons are cited by the respondents on the above issue. Among these reasons, a vast majority of all the categories (75.11%) cite that the present venture yields them only inadequate income and no profit. It is followed by 12 per cent of the respondents who report that domestic responsibilities are the major factors which restrict them from the expansion of the present business. Only 1 per cent report that the present one is enough and they do not want further expansion of business.

Table 4.43

Opinion of respondents about the Involvement of Women in Small and Micro Enterprises

Sl. No.	Opinions		Strongly Agree	Agree	Disagree	Total
1.	Entrepreneurship in small business is a boon to womenfolk	Frequency	384	52	14	450
		%	85.3	11.6	3.1	100
2.	Success in entrepreneurial career results in negligence of family and children	Frequency	399	41	10	450
		%	88.7	9.1	2.2	100
3.	Policy provision for micro enterprise not sufficient	Frequency	397	51	2	450
		%	88.2	11.3	0.4	100
4.	Right place for micro enterprise is only home	Frequency	396	49	5	450
		%	88.0	10.9	1.1	100

There are four major opinions assessed with regard to the involvement of women in micro enterprise sector. The opinions are in the areas like women empowerment, work life balance, policy provisions, and location of business. The opinion for entrepreneurship in small business is boon for women has been strongly agreed by 85.3 per cent and 11.6 per cent just agreed, whilst only 3.1 per cent have disagreed with such opinion. The major issue like work life imbalance is a major concern and it is reflected in their opinions. Nearly 89 per cent have strongly agreed that their success in business is due to the base fact that they neglect their family and children. Only 2.2 per cent of them have disagreed and 9.1 per cent have the modest agreement with of the statement.

Majority of the women have reported that the financial support of the government is not adequate to run the business and it is showed in their opinion with regard to the policy provisions. Only less than one per cent of the respondents disagree whilst, 88.2 per cent have strongly agreed and 11.3 per cent have modest agreement. In the case of location of the enterprise, 88 per cent have opined that the right place for small business is only home since they can accomplish and attend to the business work while their presence at home can make the family members happy. Nearly 11 per cent have modest agreement and only 1.1 per cent have disagreed with the statement.

Table 4.44

Distribution of Respondents According to the Kind of Advice to New Entrants

Sl. No.	Kind of Advice		Trade	Manufac-turing	Service	Total
1.	Start up with sound knowledge	Frequency	127	97	35	259
		%	54.3	77.0	38.9	57.6
2.	Involve totally	Frequency	67	12	43	122
		%	28.6	9.5	47.8	27.11
3.	Dare not to enter	Frequency	28	15	10	53
		%	12.0	11.9	11.1	11.78
4.	Nothing to say	Frequency	12	2	2	16
		%	5.1	1.6	2.2	3.56
	Total	Frequency	234	126	90	450
		%	100	100	100	100

The respondents of the study have been asked to give their feedback and their stand to advice the new entrants who intend to start the micro enterprises. It has been observed from table 4.44 that a majority of them (57.6%) have positive inclination towards this business but they advise the new comers to start up with sound knowledge as they have to encounter serious and vital economic issues and problems.

Next to it, nearly 27 per cent have strong and positive mind to invite the new entrants, who are strongly advised that this traditional venture gives absolute hope for the women to come up in life. On the contrary a few respondents (11.8%) advise not to step into the business at all, whilst 3.6 per cent have made no comments on this matter concerned.

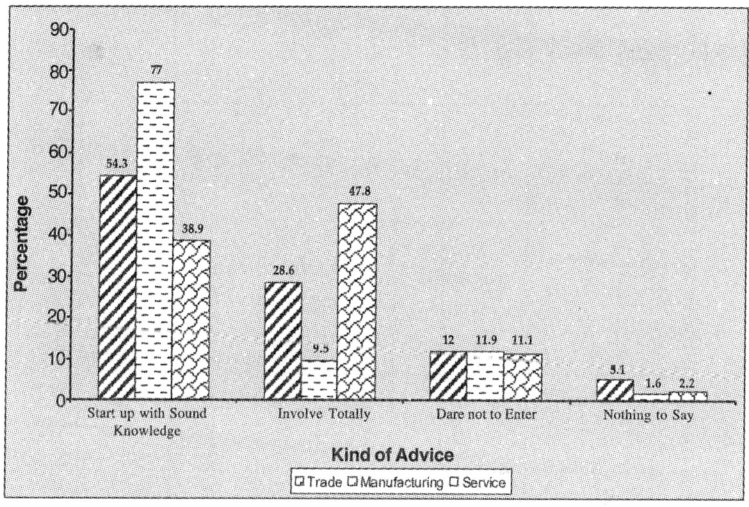

Fig. 4.35: Percentage Distribution of Respondents According to the kind of Advice to New Entrants

CROSS TABULATION ANALYSIS

In this section an attempt is made to compare the responses and analyse the relationship between responses of two different variables of the study. The cross tabulation technique establishes interdependent relationship between two tables of values, which is also called two-way tabulation.

A cross tabulation analysis has been exercised to compare the start- up capital with the occupational background of the respondents. It has been found that, among the background of professionals, nearly 67 per cent have started the business with their savings and the support of SHG finance and the remaining 33 per cent have started the business by their own savings only.

Table 4.45

Comparison Between Start-Up Capital and Occupational Background of Respondents

Sl. No.	Start-up Capital/ Occupational Background		Occupational Background				Total
			Professional	Business	Labour	Farmer	
1.	Savings by respondent only	Frequency	2	28	58	2	90
		%	33.3	25.2	28.3	1.6	20.0
2.	Finance by SHG only	Frequency	0	14	27	35	76
		%	.0	12.6	13.2	27.3	16.9
3.	Saving and SHG finance	Frequency	4	62	112	87	265
		%	66.7	55.9	54.6	68.0	58.9
4.	Borrowing from SHG and own amount	Frequency	0	3	6	2	11
		%	.0	2.7	2.9	1.6	2.4
5.	SHG and other finance sources	Frequency	0	4	2	2	8
		%	.0	3.6	1.0	1.6	1.8
	Total	Frequency	6	111	205	128	450
		%	100.0%	100.0	100.0	100.0	100.0

The respondents, who have got the background of business, reveal that a majority of them (55.9%) start the business with their savings and SHG finance. Others do it by their own savings (25.2%), finance by SHG only (12.6 per cent), SHG and other finance (3.6%) and borrowing plus SHG support (2.7%). Similar type of comparison has been done among the respondents who have the occupational background as labourers. The table shows that nearly 55 per cent of the respondents' source of finance is savings and SHG support of finance. Next to it, 28 per cent have started their ventures with the savings of the entrepreneurs only. In case of farmers, a vast majority (68.0%) of the respondents have started the business by their savings and SHG support. Next to it 27 per cent of entrepreneur's source of finance is from SHG support only. It has been found from the above analysis, that the sources of finance for all the four occupational background of the respondents are own savings and SHG support of finance.

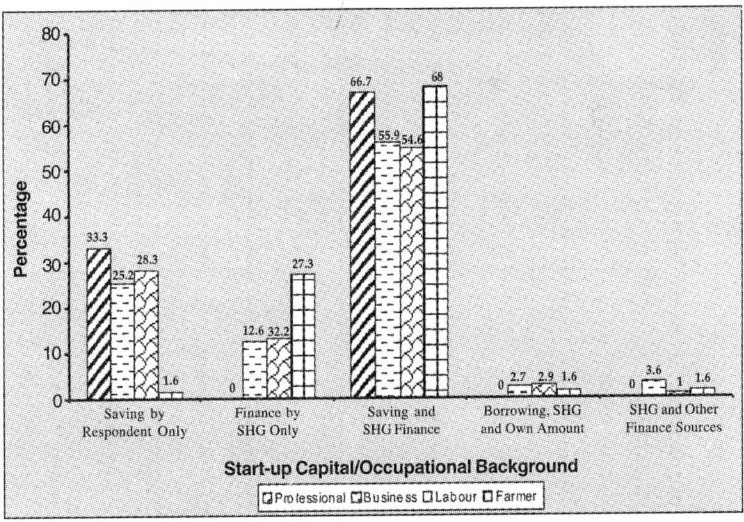

Fig. 4.36: Percentage Comparison Between Start-Up Capital and Occupational Background of Respondents

Table 4.46

Comparison Between Motivational Factors with Previous Occupation of Respondents

Sl. No.	Motivational Factors/ Occupation before Entrepreneurship		House Wife	Student	Employee	Family Business	Social Worker	Total
1	2		3	4	5	6	7	8
1.	Making money/profit	Frequency	113	4	14	10	0	141
		%	25.1	0.9	3.1	2.2	.0	31.3
2.	Want control and freedom	Frequency	1	0	8	0	0	9
		%	.2	.0	1.8	.0	.0	2.0
3.	Self Reliance	Frequency	36	0	99	1	12	138
		%	8.0	.0	22.0	.2	0.4	30.7
4.	To make own decisions	Frequency	10	0	13	0	0	24
		%	2.2	.0	2.9	.0	.0	5.3
5.	Better social status	Frequency	7	0	7	1	0	15
		%	1.6	.0	1.6	.2	.0	3.3

(Table Contd...)

1	2		3	4	5	6	7	8
6.	Self achievement	Frequency	36	1	74	2	0	113
		%	8.0	.2	16.4	.4	.0	25.1
7.	Threat of losing job	Frequency	4	0	1	0	0	5
		%	.9	.0	.2	.0	.0	1.1
8.	Family circumstance	Frequency	0	0	1	1	0	2
		%	.0	.0	.2	.2	.0	.4
9.	Giving employment to others	Frequency	2	0	0	0	0	2
		%	.4	.0	.0	.0	.0	.4
10.	Own business	Frequency	210	5	217	15	3	450
		%	46.7	1.1	48.2	3.3	.7	100.0

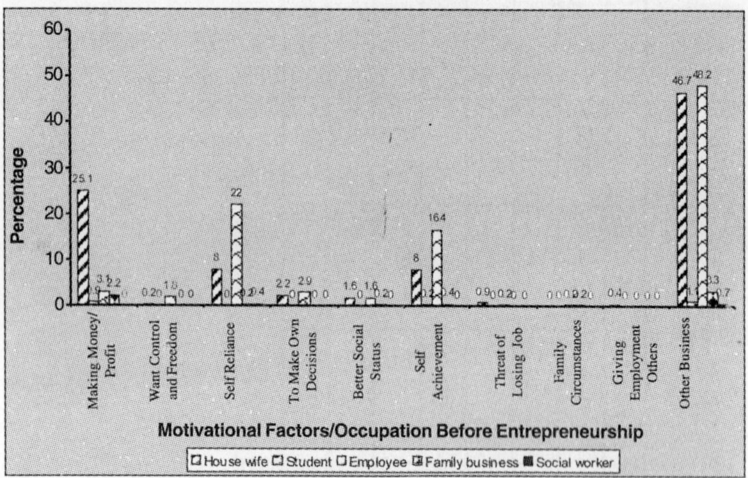

Fig. 4.37: Percentage Comparison Between Motivational Factors with Previous Occupation of Respondents

The analysis on the basis of previous occupational background of the respondents show that, the choice by the housewives goes this money and profit (25.1%), control and freedom (8%), and self achievement (8%). The motivations of entrepreneurs who are students are making money and profit (0.9%) which is found to be highest. The employee's options are want and control and freedom (22.0%), self achievement (16.4%). The women, who are in family business, opt for making money and profit (2.2%) and own business (2.2%). Only 0.7 per cent of the social workers' option is to have control and freedom by doing business.

Table 4.47 compares the occupational status of the respondents before their self employment and their idea for starting the enterprise. The purpose of this comparison is to understand the different sections of entrepreneurs who have had the inspiration to start the business.

It reveals that a vast majority of housewives (71.90%) have started their business from the advice of their family members.

Table 4.47

Comparison of Occupations of the Respondents before their Entrepreneurship and Idea given to Start

Sl. No.	Occupation Before Entrepreneurship/Idea to Start		House Wife	Student	Employee	Family Business	Social Worker
1.	Advice from family	Frequency	151	2	213	0	3
		%	71.60	40.0	98.15	-	100%
2.	Inherited from the past	Frequency	18	1	2	14	0
		%	8.57	20	0.9	93.33	.0
3.	Success stories	Frequency	1	0	0	0	0
		%	0.47	–	–	–	–
4.	SHG recommendation	Frequency	33	2	1	1	0
		%	15.71	40	0.45	6.46	–
5.	Others	Frequency	7	0	1	0	0
		%	3.33	-	0.45	–	–
	Total	Frequency	210	5	217	15	3
		%	100	100	100	100	100

Of these groups, nearly 16 per cent have started their business by the recommendation of SHG, whereas 8.57 have taken over the business from the strength of the property of their concerned as a background household. A poor performance has been recorded that only 0.4 per cent has started their business by seeing the success stories of others. Among the employees, a close to cent per cent (98.15%) have started their business with their family members. The respondents of the study who were students before their self employment have shown that an equal of 40 per cent have got the idea from the advice and recommendations of the family members and SHGs. 93.33 per cent of the women entrepreneurs who were doing other family business earlier continue the present ones. All the respondents, who are the social activists, have got inspiration to start the business with their family members or of their own.

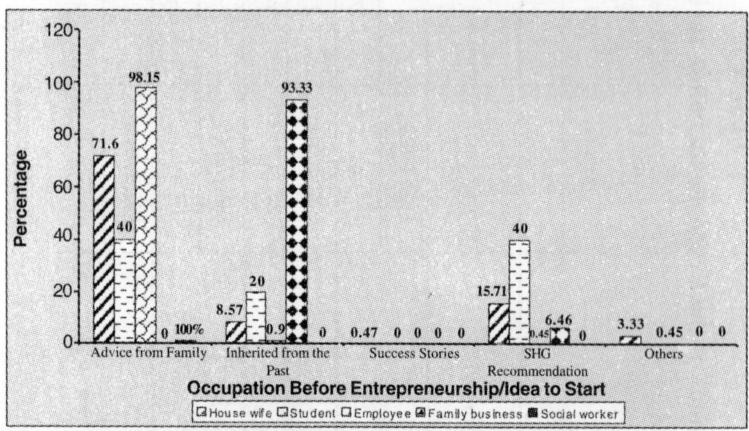

Fig. 4.38: Percentage Comparison of Occupations of the Respondents before their Entrepreneurship and Idea given to Start

A comparison has been worked out between the variables of location of business enterprise and the volume of sales per month. It reveals that 57.97 per cent of the women, who earn up to Rs 10,000 per month, are highly concentrated and operate their business from their own house. 25.50 per cent of the women run the business at the stalls in the market.

Table 4.48

Comparison of Location of Business and Sales Volume

Sl. No.	Location of Business/Sales Volume		Upto Rs. 10000	Rs. 10001 to 20000	Rs. 20001 to 30000	Above 30000	Total
1.	Own house	Frequency	200	55	8	1	264
		%	57.97	63.95	47.05	50	–
2.	Stall at the market	Frequency	88	8	5	–	101
		%	25.50	9.30	29.41	–	–
3.	Shop specifically allotted for business	Frequency	42	22	3	–	67
		%	12.17	25.58	17.64		–
4.	Land specifically allotted for business	Frequency	6	0	1	–	7
		%	0.17	–	5.88	–	–
5.	Others	Frequency	9	1	0	1	11
		%	2.60	1.11	–	50	–
	Total	Frequency	345	86	17	2	450
		%	100	100	100	100	100

Only a few respondents of the above sale volume have got other locations. As in the above, nearly 64 per cent of respondents, who have the sale volume ranging between Rs 10000 to 20000, operate the business from their house. However 25.58 per cent of the respondents of this category have established their shop specifically allotted to them for the business. The location of business of women, whose turnover of sales ranges between Rs20000 to Rs 30000 was found in their own house, (47.05%) followed by stall in the market (29.4%) shop specifically allotted for their business (17.64%). The above analysis reveals that a vast majority of the women entrepreneurs in all the category of sales volume run and operate own business from their house. It is really disappointing to note that the other important locations for business such as stall and shop in business places are not a major location for micro enterprises.

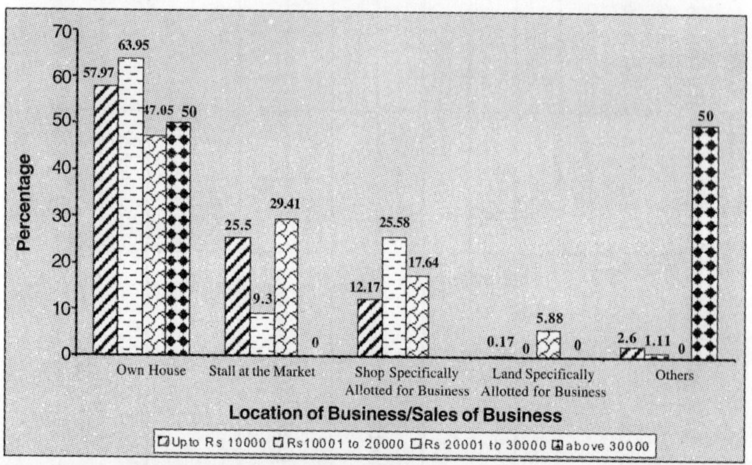

Fig. 4.39: Percentage Comparison of Location of Business and Sales Volume

RELIABILITY AND FACTOR ANALYSIS FOR MOTIVATION OF BUSINESS

Reliability Analysis

The reliability of scales, which is used in this study, has been calculated by Cronbach's coefficient alpha. Cronbach's alpha reliability coefficient normally ranges between 0 and 1. However, there is actually no lower limit to the coefficient. The closer Cronbach's alpha coefficient is to 1.0 the greater the internal consistency of the items in the scale. The coefficient alpha value exceeds the minimum standard of .70. It has provided good estimates of internal consistency reliability.

- The formula is as follows:

$$\alpha = \frac{kr}{1 + (k - 1)\, r}$$

- K is the number of items in the scale.
- R is the average correlation pairs of items.
- As the number of items in the scale (k) increases, the value of alpha becomes larger.
- If the inter-correlation between items is large, the corresponding alpha will also be larger.

As shown in Table 4.49 coefficient alpha values ranged from .550 to .698 for all the constructs. All constructs obtained an acceptable level of a coefficient alpha above .70, indicating that the scales used in this study were reliable. While increasing the value of alpha is partially dependent on the number of items in the scale, it should be noted that this has diminishing returns. It should also be noted that an alpha of 0.7 is probably a reasonable goal. It should also be noted that while a high value for Cronbach's alpha indicates good internal consistency of the items in the scale, it does not mean that the scale is undimensional. Factor analysis is a method to determine the dimensionality of the above scale.

Factor Analysis

(a) Motivational Factors For Small Business and Micro-Enterprise by Women Entrepreneurs

Factor Analysis is a set of technique, used to analyse the correlations between variables and reduce their numbers into fewer factors, which explain much of the original data more economically. Even though a subjective interpretation can result

Table 4.49

Reliability of Scales and Item-Construct Loadings – Factors Related to Motivation for Small Business

Sl. No.	Items	Mean	Standard	Scale Mean if Item Deleted	Cronbach's Alpha if Item Deleted
1.	Making money/profit	4.0022	.65562	39.5222	.692
2.	Self Reliance	3.9378	.75841	39.5867	.698
3.	Want control and freedom	4.0000	.65051	39.5244	.683
4.	To make my own decisions	3.9844	.65203	39.5400	.653
5.	Better social status	3.9978	.64879	39.5267	.651
6.	Self achievement	3.9867	.65719	39.5378	.691
7.	Threat of loosing job	3.9933	.65218	39.5311	.570
8.	Family circumstances	3.9533	.75512	39.5711	.573
9.	Giving employment to others	3.9333	.73111	39.5911	.600
10.	Own business	3.8622	.85138	39.6622	.550
11.	Any other reasons	3.8733	.88765	39.6511	.550
	Mean				**43.52**
	Variance				**14.783**
	Standard Deviation				**3.766**
	Cronbach's Alpha				**0.7**
	No of Items				**11**

from a factor analysis output, the procedure often provides an insight into the relevant psychographic variables, and results in economic use of data collection efforts. The subjective element of factor analysis is reduced by splitting the sample randomly into two and extracting factors separately from both parts. If similar factors result, the analysis is assumed as reliable or stable. (Nargundkar Rajendra, 2003)

(b) Methods of conducting Factor Analysis

There are two stages in factor analysis.

Stage 1: Factor Extraction process,- this process is primarily used to determine how many factors will be extracted from data.

Stage 2: Rotation of Principal Components.-This is actually optional, but highly recommended. In this study, the rotation of principal component is used. After extracting the factors, the next task is to interpret and title the relevant factors. This is done by the process of identifying factors, associated with the original variables. The factor matrix is used for this purpose. The rotated factor matrix comes about in stage 2. This is used to anlayse and interprets the factors.

The factor matrix gives us the loading of each variable on each of the extracted factors. This is similar to a correlation matrix with 'loadings' have values between 0 and 1. Values close to 1 represent high loadings and those close to 0, denote low loadings. The normal procedure is to identify the high loading factors and provide a suitable title.

(c) Steps involved in conducting Factor Analysis

The steps involved in conducting factor analysis are as follows:

- The first step is to formulate the factor analysis problem and identify the variables to be factor analyzed.
- The next step is to develop a correlation matrix of the variables and the method of factor analysis is selected.
- The next step involves the researcher's decision on extraction of number of factors and the method of rotation.

- Next, the rotated factors should be interpreted.
- Depending on the objective, the factor scores may be calculated, or surrogate variables selected to represent the factors in subsequent multivariate analysis

(d) Statistics Associated with Factor Analysis

Formal statistics are available for testing the appropriateness of the factor model.

1. Bartlett's test of sphericity

Bartlett's test of sphericity is used to test the null hypothesis that the variables are uncorrelated in the population. The test for sphericity is based on a chi- square transformation of the determinant of the correlation matrix. A large value of the test statistics favours the rejection of the null hypothesis.

2. Kaiser-Meyer-Olkin measure of sampling adequacy

This index compares the magnitude of the observed correlation coefficients to the magnitude of the partial correlation coefficients. Small values indicate that the correlations between pairs of variables cannot be explained by other variables and that factor analysis will not be appropriate.

3. Eigen value

It represents the total variance explained by each factor.

4. Factor loading

Simple correlation between the variables and the factors.

5. Factor matrix

Contains the factor loadings of all the variables and the factors.

(e) Motivational factors for Small Business Entrepreneurs

Kaiser-Meyer-Olkin Measure of Sampling Adequacy (KMO) & Bartlett's Test of Sphericity have been applied to test whether the relationship among the variables has been significant or not.

Table 4.50

KMO AND Bartlett's Test

Kaiser-Meyer-Olkin Measure of Sampling Adequacy - **0.805**		
Bartlett's test of sphericity	Approx Chi-Square	2213.407
	Df	55
	Sig.	.000

Table 4.50 represents the values of approximate chi-square by Bartlett's test of Sphericity with 55 degree of freedom, which is found to be 2213.407. Since this value is significant at 0.00, so reject the null hypothesis that the population correlation matrix is an identity matrix. This means that there exists a correlation among the variables X^1, X^2 ...X^7 The value of KMO is found to be 0.805 which is more than 0.5. So, factor analysis is an appropriate technique to analyze the data.

It can be seen from table 4.51 shows the factors loadings to major obstacles in running the business. It indicates the Rotated Component Matrix wherein rotation converged in iterations. Using the Rotated Component Matrix which is a better matrix for interpreting factors, the factors are interpreted as explained below;

Factor 1, the variables like Making money /profit, Self achievement, Giving employment to others, Family circumstances and Threat of losing my job have high loading on factor 1 due to high correlation values of 0.906 , 0.898, 0.885, 0.856 and 0.823. On *Factor 2*, the variables like "Self reliance" and "Own business" have high loading on factor 2 due to high correlation values of 0.904 and 0.879. On *Factor 3*. The variables like "Want control and freedom" and "To make my own decisions" have high loading on factor 3 due to high correlation values of 0.758 and 0.711, and *Factor 4*, the variables like any other reasons and Better social status have high loading on factor 3 due to high correlation values of .856 and 0.631.

Table 4.51

Loading of Motivational Factors for Small Business Entrepreneurs

No.	Variables	Factor I	Factor II	Factor III	Factor IV
X^1	Making money/profit	.906	.015	-.045	-.020
X^6	Self achievement	.898	-.114	.025	-.045
X^9	Giving employment to others	.885	-.067	-.006	.107
X^8	Family circumstances	.856	-.189	-.015	-.013
X^7	Threat of losing job	.823	.022	.172	-.017
X^2	Self Reliance	-.077	.904	-.006	-.060
X^{10}	Own business	-.130	.879	-.055	-.020
X^3	Want control and freedom	-.091	-.248	.758	-.065
X^4	To make own decisions	.120	.144	.711	.156
X^{11}	Any other reasons	-.112	-.131	-.112	.856
X^5	Better social status	.126	.065	.361	.631
	Eigan values	3.987	1.711	1.362	1.019
	Variance (in%)	36.250	15.552	12.383	9.261
	Cumulative Eigan values (in)	36.250	51.802	64.185	73.445

Extraction Method: Principal Component Analysis.

Rotation Method: Varimax with Kaiser Normalization.

Factor Extraction Process was performed by Principal Component Analysis to identify the number of factors to be extracted from the data and by specifying the most commonly used Varimax rotation method. In the principal component analysis, total variance in the data is considered.

Table 4.52

Motivational factors for Small Business Entrepreneurs–Communalities

Sl.No.	Variables	Initial	Extraction (C^2)
X^1	Making money/profit	1.000	0.823
X^2	Self reliance	1.000	0.827
X^3	Want control and freedom	1.000	0.649
X^4	To make own decisions	1.000	0.565
X^5	Better social status	1.000	0.549
X^6	Self achievement	1.000	0.822
X^7	Threat of losing job	1.000	0.708
X^8	Family circumstances	1.000	0.769
X^9	Giving employment to others	1.000	0.799
X^{10}	Own business	1.000	0.793
X^{11}	Any other reasons	1.000	0.775

Extraction Method: Principal Component Analysis.

The above table shows the proportion of the variance explained by the six factors in each variable. The proportion of variance is explained by the common factors called communalities of the variance. Principal Component Analysis works on initial assumption that all the variance is common. Therefore, before extraction the communalities are all 1.000. Then the most common approach for determining the number of factors to retain, i.e., examining Eigen values was done. Under "communalities", "Initial" column can be seen that communality for each variable X^1 to X^{11} is 1.0 as unities were inserted in the diagonals of the correlation matrix. The c^2 ^{S}represent the communalities column. This is the amount of variance a variable shares with all other variables being considered with all the variables to the extent of more than seventy per cent. The importance of a given variable can exactly be expressed in terms of the variations in the variable than can be accounted for by the factor.

It is concluded that based on the factor analysis, the variables namely "making money and profit" "Self-achievement" and "Self reliance" are the most important success factors for motivation of small business and micro enterprises by poor and marginalized section of women since these factors significantly emerge higher than the other variables.

RELIABILITY AND WEIGHTED AVERAGE SCORE ANALYSIS ON MAJOR OBSTACLES IN RUNNING THE BUSINESS

Reliability Analysis

From the table 4.53 coefficient alpha values range from .928 to .936 for all the constructs. All constructs obtained an acceptable level of a coefficient alpha above .70, indicating that the scales used in this study were reliable. While increasing the value of alpha is partially dependent upon the number of items in the scale, it should be noted that this has diminishing returns. It should be noted that an alpha of 0.940 is probably a reasonable goal. It should also be noted that while a high value for Cronbach's alpha indicates good internal consistency of the items in the scale, it does not mean that the scale is unidimensional. The above scale items are eligible for further analysis.

Weighted Average Score on Major Obstacles in Running the Business

The weighted average score analysis deals with the respondents' agreeability over the pros and cons of the problem faced while running the business. The seven factors are considered in the group. For the purpose of analysis five point scaling technique was used to convert the qualitative information into quantitative one. For the agreeability levels the score is assigned. In this section, the results are given in the following tables with suitable interpretations.

Table 4.53

Reliability of Scales and Item-Construct Loadings-Factors Related to Major Obstacles in Running the Business

Sl.No.	Items	Mean	Std.	Corrected Item-Total Correlation	Cronbach's Alpha If Item Deleted
1.	Coordinating family and work life	3.798	.9375	.766	.936
2.	Liquidity and other financial problems	3.971	.7381	.805	.930
3.	No time for training to upgrade skills	4.004	.6539	.796	.932
4.	Gaining the acceptance and respect of people	3.940	.7601	.808	.930
5.	Problems related with raw material	3.938	.7315	.844	.927
6.	Problems related to marketing the product	3.856	.8568	.819	.929
7.	No obstacles	3.864	.8963	.829	.928
	Mean				27.3711
	Variance				23.152
	Standard Deviation				4.81160
	Cronbach's Alpha Based on Standardized Items				.943
	Cronbach's Alpha				.940
	No. of Items				7

Table 4.54

Ranking the Problem Faced by the Respondents on the Major Obstacles in Running the Business

Sl. No.	Factors	Total Score	Mean Score	Rank
1.	Coordinating family and work life	1739	3.86	I
2.	Liquidity and other financial problems	1629	3.62	VI
3.	No time for training to upgrade skills	1723	3.83	II
4.	Gaining the acceptance and respect of people	1673	3.72	IV
5.	Problems related with raw material	1632	3.63	V
6.	Problems related to marketing the product	1696	3.77	III
7.	No obstacles	1584	3.52	VII

The above table 4.54 reveals the ranking of the problems faced by the respondents while running the business. 'Combining family and work life' was ranked first by the selected sample respondents with the total score of 1739 and mean score of 3.86. 'No time for training to upgrade skills' was ranked second by the selected sample respondents with the total score of 1723 and mean score of 3.83. 'Problems related to marketing the product' was ranked third with the total score of 1696 and mean score of 3.77. 'Gaining the acceptance/ respect of people' occupied fourth position with the total score of 1673 and mean score of 3.72. 'Problems related with raw material' occupied fifth position with the total score of 1632 and mean score of 3.63. 'Liquidity and other financial problems' occupied six positions with the total score of 1629 and mean score of 3.62. 'No obstacles' was in the last position with the total score of 1584 and mean score of 3.52. It is evident that most of the respondents gave top priority to combining family and work life as the first rank for ranking of the problems faced by the respondents while running the business.

Garrett Ranking Technique for Major Obstacles in Starting the Business

This technique was used to rank the preference of the respondents on different aspects of the study. The order of merit given by the respondents were converted into ranks by using the following formula.:

$$\text{Percentage Position} = \frac{100\,(R_{ij} - 0.5)}{N_j}$$

Where R_{ij} = Rank given for i^{th} factor by j^{th} individual

N_j = Number of factors ranked by j^{th} individual

The percentage position of each rank thus obtained is converted into scores by referring to the table given by Henry E.Garret (2004). Then for each factor, the scores of individual respondents are added together and divided by the total number of respondents for whom the scores were added. These mean scores for all the factors were arranged in the descending order, ranks given and most important aspects identified.

Table 4.55 reveals the ranking of the problems faced by the respondents at the time of start the business. "Start up finance" was ranked first by the selected sample respondents with the total score of 25768 and mean score of 57.26. "Family and work life" was ranked second by the selected sample respondents with the total score of 25204 and mean score of 56.01. "Gender discrimination" was ranked third with the total score of 23780 and mean score of 52.84. "Question of self confidence" occupied the fourth, position with the total score of 22976 and mean score of 51.06. "Any other reasons" occupied the fifth position with the total score of 22006 and mean score of 48.90. "Lack of information/advice" was in the six positions with the total score of 20902 and mean score of 46.45. "Management skills" held the next position with the total score of 20760 and mean score of 46.13. "No obstacles" occupied the last position with the total score of 18778 and mean score of 41.73. It is evident that most of the respondents gave top priority to start up finance while ranking of the problems faced by the respondents at the time of starting the business.

Table 4.55

Rank the Problems Faced by the Respondents at the Time of Starting the Business

Sl. No.	Factors	Total Score	Mean Score	Rank
1.	Question of self confidence	22976	51.06	IV
2.	Start up finance	25768	57.26	I
3.	Lack of information/advice	20902	46.45	VI
4.	Management skills	20760	46.13	VII
5.	Gender discrimination	23780	52.84	III
6.	Family and work life	25204	56.01	II
7.	Any other reasons	22006	48.90	V
8.	No obstacles	18778	41.73	VIII

REFERENCES

1. Henry E.Garrett,(2004) "Statistics in Psychology and Education, Vakils, Feffer and Simsons, Bombay.
2. Nargundkar, Rajendra,(2003) "Marketing Research- Text and Cases", Tata McGraw Hill, New Delhi, pp. 312-313.

5

Suggestions and Conclusion

INTRODUCTION

This chapter summarizes the study as a whole. The major findings of the analysis of the issues of women entrepreneurship in small business and micro enterprises are presented in this section. Further suggestions are also offered for the development of the women entrepreneurs and devising strategies to policy makers and government.

Women in micro enterprises and small business is a new area of women entrepreneurship for investigation in the socio-economic environment in India. The perspective of women, particularly in rural area, is gradually changing with the growing sensitivity of the roles, responsibilities and social and economic status of the women in the society in general and family in particular due to their involvement in micro enterprise sector. At the same time the process of starting and operating a new enterprise is tremendously difficult and involves considerable risk, especially in traditional sector. Women often lack management skills, education, inadequate family and societal support system to facilitate their efforts.

Reviews of literature have made it evident that few studies have been conducted on women entrepreneurship in micro enterprises, studying different entrepreneurial aspects at different geographical areas. The nature of problem experienced by women entrepreneurs in micro enterprise sector in Coimbatore District in Tamilnadu was thought to be an area yet less explored and motivated to conceptualize the present research. It would be quite pertinent that a research study is carried out in this district to examine the real time issues faced by the women entrepreneurs in small business and micro enterprises, especially women who belong to Self Help Groups (SHG) in Tamilnadu. The study looks at the various aspects of issues of women such as work life imbalance, marketing, finance, future aspirations etc.

The major objectives of the study are:

1. To review the profile of women entrepreneurs in small business and micro enterprises.
2. To explore the problems of women entrepreneurs in balancing household chores and business responsibilities.
3. To identify the various economic issues unique to women in setting up and running the business and enterprise.
4. To give remedial measures for the effective performance of women entrepreneurship in small business and micro enterprises.

The women entrepreneurs who belong to Self Help Groups (SHG) in the Taluks of Palladam, Pollachi and Udumalpet Taluk of Coimbatore District, TamilNadu are the sample respondents of this study. Multi Stage sampling technique has been adopted. In the first stage 3 Taluks were taken for the study. In the second stage 75 SHGs were identified, each Taluk covering 25 SHGs. In the third stage 450 SHG members, holding different categories of small business and micro enterprise, have been randomly chosen as the sample for the study. The present study is empirical in nature and has been studied mainly by primary data. The secondary data have been used to a limited extent as the selected topic is explanatory in nature. The supporting data were collected from the collector's office, official records of SHGs etc.

MAJOR FINDINGS

Demographic and Business Profile of Respondents

The age of the respondents highlights the fact that nearly fifty per cent of the respondents are in the age between 31 and 40. A vast majority (67%) belongs to the backward class community. It has been found that 92 per cent of the respondents are living with common law. No spinster has been found in the study. With respect of the number family members, nearly 87 per cent of the respondent's family size consists of four to six members.

The lowest level of educational status was found among the respondents. Nearly three fifth the of respondents have completed only primary school level, whereas only 1.3 per cent of respondents have obtained degree/diploma. A simple majority of the respondents belong to the group named labourers in farm/non- farm family background and next to it, agricultural background. Past work experience reveals that a majority of the respondent's nature of occupation was having been employees in an organisation. Some of them are housewives.

It is surprising to note that three fifths of the respondents' location of business is their own house. Nearly fifty per cent are doing the business individually without the support of anybody else. It has been found that employment opportunity in these ventures is found to be minimal. In case for initial investment in business, a vast majority of the respondent's investment in business is found to be less than one lakh. In the aspect of start-up capital, majority of the respondents have started the business with their own savings along with the financial support of the concerned SHGs.

Background Information about Motivational factors

An overwhelming majority of respondents have been given idea/advice by the respective family members to start the enterprise. Among the ten motivational factors, three factors emerged high such as making money and profit (31.3%), self-reliance (30.7%) and self achievement (25.1%).

Issues Related to Starting and Running the Enterprise by Women

Among the various reasons for having chosen the traditional business, it was not surprising to find that nearly two -third of them answered that they did not want to take risk. The reasons attributed are that since the investment level is low combined with low education, it leads to low self confidence, and self- reliance which makes the women engage in traditional business. More than ninety per cent of the respondents do not undergo the initial ground work such as preparation of business plan, attending EDPs and testing the sample product in market place for the typical business at the time of start.

Except 0.7 per cent for the respondents, a close to cent per cent (99.3%) of them reported that they had the obstacles while they were starting the business. It was found that question of combining work and family was the foremost psychological problem of start up as well as running the business.

It has been found that for a vast majority of respondents (96.9%) average number of working days is from 11 to 20 days. The reason for low concentration on days and hours of work is their inability to balance between domestic responsibilities and business activities.

Issues Related to Marketing of Business by Women Entrepreneurs

Method of marketing to influence the customer is not a necessary one because of their nature of product like tailoring shop, small hotels and intermediary products to supply to other small enterprises pointed out by nearly 50 per cent of the total respondents. Similarly a number of respondents point out that as their business is done in their own house, they do not want publicity to their product. The analysis also shows that nearly 84 per cent of the total respondents' sale of the product is directly to the customers, coming to their shop.

Collection of payment for the sale of the product of micro enterprises run by the women is found to be a major issue. A vast majority of respondents (86.2%) reported that their major problems arise from the male customers. Almost all the respondents in all the categories had acknowledged that the demand for the product was facing fluctuation. There were two major reasons cited by the respondents. Maximum of the respondents (99.3%) quoted the competitive challenge emanating from the organized sector product.

Issues Related to Loan for Micro Enterprises Run by Women

Nearly fifty per cent of respondents have availed the loan from commercial banks. However, a vast majority of the respondents reported that they had to meet difficulties in getting the loans. The difficulties were mainly in the form of delay in crediting the amount. The co-operative banks and NBFCs also play a significant role by extending financial help to the respondents of the study.

With regard to present position of loan, a vast majority of respondents (85.11%) have already started repaying the loan but could settle only part of the amount. There are various reasons cited by the respondents for the delay in repaying the debt. Among the reasons nearly fifty per cent of the respondents acknowledged that the income from the business is diverted for household purposes.

Issues Related to Skill Acquisition for Business

All the members have received a formal training by SHGs. Of them one-fourth have acknowledged that the concerned training was only a small step and the source of skill acquisition. The main driving force for their skill acquisition other than typical training is by Mahalir Thittam. Nearly 40 have per cent have gained knowledge from actual business practices.

Issues Related to Balancing Household Chores and Business Work

Fifty per cent of the women have reported that their family members have been the well wishers and encourage them to do the business but they do not actively engage themselves in business activities. On the contrary, nearly 30 per cent of the study respondents have not received any support from their family members and they have to meet the challenges on their own.

There is a major positive response from the families of women entrepreneurs towards the attitudinal change after the successful running of the business. Nearly three fifth of the husbands of these entrepreneurs have turned to become supporters. It also shows that among the family members the support spouse is much appreciable. The husband's support is found to be highly strong in the area of purchasing materials (56.7 %), for the business.

The impact of business activities reveals that a vast majority of the respondents in all the categories, viz Trade, Manufacturing and Service have experienced negative change because of their activities towards household chores such as household work including child care, attending sleeping hours etc.,

Business Success and Future Aspirations of Women Entrepreneurs

Among the five factors for analyzing the level of success, a few per cent of respondents have revealed negative expression about their business. Only 0.9 per cent of the total respondents have the intention to close their business. It is found that the business is to fulfill their desirable level and they do business to remain in it.

The performance activities have been rated by the respondents. It is really appreciable that in the aspect of financial benefits 78 per cent of the respondents feel good, whilst the aspect of work life balance has been rated well by 34 per cent of women respondents. The aspect of development of communication skill shows that a vast majority of them (86%) rate it as good, the ability to use their initiatives as good (70%) and social upliftment has been rated good by 69 per cent of respondents.

Nearly three fifth of the respondents distribute their revenue arising from their business to repay the loan, but it is disappointing that only one fourth per cent of them invest the revenue and plough them back in the same business for further expansion.

The reasons for dissatisfaction on business have been assessed in the study. Among the economic reasons, lack of finance and equipment and poor income generation are the causable factors, whilst on the non-economic factors, stress in business, issue related to work life imbalance are the major reasons. In spite of the women entrepreneurs facing several issues as per this study, their attitude towards holding on to the business is quite optimistic; nearly two –third of the women want to continue the business. But it is disappointing that a vast majority (88%) are not willing or unable to go for further expansion of business.

Their feedback and their stand to advice the new entrants who intend to start the micro enterprises reveals the fact that a majority of them (57.6%) have positive inclination to this business but they advise the new comers to come out with sound knowledge as they have to encounter serious and vital economic issues and problems.

SUGGESTIONS

Based on the findings and views expressed by the respondents, the following suggestions have been made to improve the socio-economic status of women entrepreneurs in small businesses and micro enterprises.

EDPs/Training/Education

- The government should come forward to organize training programmes to educate the aspirants who wish to start their own business. Awareness programme in such business endeavors should be organized for the benefit of the economically backward community.
- As the women in micro enterprises hail from economically weaker families they meet problems such as lack of enthusiasm, motivation and support from spouse and

other family members. The SHGs under the aegis of Mahalir Thittam may give the women entrepreneurs personal counselling by way of organizing Entrepreneurial Development Programmes (EDP) to make them more confident women entrepreneurs. Resource persons from small scale industries, DIC, Technical Educational Institutions may be invited for such programmes.

- As the women have poor educational background and so do the family members, they invariably lack knowledge in the field of book -keeping, accounts maintances and other financial matters relating to business and enterprises. Hence training in these areas is also to be given to enhance the managerial competency of these entrepreneurs.
- The training programme offered by the office of the Mahalir Thittam at the dawn of the enterprise or business venture is conventionally typical. After that no follow up exercise has been initiated. Since many of the women belonged to marginalized group, the access to enhancement of skill through training is not possible. It is suggested that training in innovative economic activities by using the resources available locally in and around the region can be given to the entrepreneurs.

Sharing of Knowledge

- Another problem of micro enterprises is the lack of net working system. It can be suggested that the women in SHGs of various geographical areas such as rural, semi-urban, and urban should have a proper networking system to share their technical information and acquire good public relationships.
- Large numbers of women entrepreneurs lack confidence to run the business. It is suggested that the head of the self help group (animator) can lead the members, operating micro enterprises, to visit to the successful enterprises in the nearby districts so that they can share their experience and knowledge for better performance.

Issues Relating to Marketing

- Marketing and selling the products is a major problem of the micro enterprising community. This vital business process destabilises the micro entrepreneurs and the net result is that they are unable to sell their products which remain a dead stock. It leads to loss of income and failure in business. It is suggested that sufficient training should be given to them in marketing methods and techniques to enhance the respondents marketing techniques, ability and skills.
- It is suggested that for selling the products of micro business community, the government and the SHGs should take steps to set up stalls in the localities wherever festivals take place. This kind of assistance is to enhance their profit margin. This is the kind of help the micro business community also expects.
- Lack of publicity is found to be the major setback for the various problems in marketing. Government should take steps to assist the group to participate in trade fair, exhibition and conference to improve the sale of the business. Moreover, they can be given assistance by offering incentives and concessions to organize awareness programmes through various communications media.

Issues Relating to Loan/Grants and Subsidies

- Procedural formalities are the reasons for the delay in obtaining the loan from the financial institutions. Efforts are necessary in the direction of simplifications of the procedures, formalities and regulations in all matters relating to the avail of bank loan. As these entrepreneurs lack the educational qualifications, the documents shall be in the form of regional language. More over the period and the number of installments for the repayment of the loan should be extended and increased.
- The members of the SHGs who obtain loan, differs in the business they do and, in their income and savings. Therefore the loan amounts they have to repay differ

from respondent to respondent. The member or the borrower expects that there should be some change in the mode of repayment. The rate of interest charged for the loans given to small business by the banks should further be reduced to save the borrowers from falling into the debt – trap.

- For enterprises that are innovative there shall be special grants and concessions or subsidies. For example, in tailoring, to enhance the productivity and income, new technology and the most sophisticated tailoring machineries have to be used. In such cases, their expenses will increase which may be strain to their borrowings. It is suggested that the government should consider granting subsidies or concessions for the successful pursuit of the business ventures.
- The Nationalised Banks and the co-operative Banks, who sanction subsidy to the SHGs, should take up the role of training the beneficiaries, to maintain accounts. Towards that, orientation course and oft repeated refresher course can be conducted.
- By a successful SHG, the economy of not only the members but also the whole nation increases. So the government should introduce pension schemes to the elderly members of the group, who have been consistent in their business. Similarly, certain exclusive medical schemes can be made available only to members of SHG. This will encourage their stability in the enterprise.

CONCLUSION

To conclude women's income in the family is very essential and important for the economic and educational upliftment of the family. Formation and participation of women in Self-Help Groups help them to develop entrepreneurial qualities, increase their employment opportunities and the horizon of their knowledge. On the whole, the women in small business and micro enterprises have become a strong driving force in the present major concern of women empowerment. Many women entrepreneurs in the study have an average age of 40-60 as they are either settled as housewives or employees in business organisations. On the one hand, their primary goal is to get monetary benefits and on the other, they have personal gratification to be self-employed. But they have to face several issues in starting as well as running the business without hitch. Although their educational background has not shown any positive effect in their business, in the long run, it will be managed as they learn the skill through their practical knowledge of business. It is hoped that with more aid of funds, training and skill development programmes from government and other non-governmental organisations, these stakeholders can be groomed to become successful entrepreneurs and contribute to the economic growth and social upliftment of our nation.

Bibliography

BOOKS

Asha Patil and Anuradha Mathu (2007) "Women *and Entrepreneurship–Issues and Challenges,* Kalpaz Publications, Delhi.

Berger M, and Byvinie .M (1989) *"Women Ventures"* West Hartford CT, Kumarian Press.

Creevey L"(1991)"*Changing Women's Lives and Work"*, Intermediate Technology Publication, London ,UK.

Haynes.G.W. (1995) *"Executive Summary: Financial Structure of Women Owned Businesses* (SBA-8029-A.93) Washington DC: Small Business Administration.

Hagen E.E (1962) *"On the Theory of Social Change: How Economic Growth Begins,* Homewood, Illinois: Dorsey.

Henry E.Garrett, (2004) "Statistics in Psychology and Education", Vakils, Feffer and Simsons, Bombay.

Hisrich R.D, Peter M.P. (1989) *" Entrepreneurship, Starting, Developing and Managing a New Enterprise"* Richard D.Irvin, Bostan.

Howrath, R (1992) "Women's Micro Enterprise – Lessens for Enterprise Support Agencies" (ed) *Development of Micro Enterprises by Women,* British Council Division.

Knight. F.(1921) *"Risk, Uncertainty and Profit"* Bostan; Houghton Mifflin.

Kausik D.S. (2009) *"Women Entrepreneurship"* Ritu Publications, Jaipur.

Mcclelland D.C. (1961) "*The Achieving Society*" Collier-Mcmillain, Toranto.

Nargundkar, Rajendra,(2003) "Marketing Research–Text and Cases", Tata McGraw Hill, New Delhi, pp. 312-313.

Nalini Shija Chanamban (2006) "*Women Entrepreneurship in North Eastern Region of India—Problems and Prospects*", Vista International Publishing House, Delhi.

Perera L. (1998) "Women in Micro and Small Scale Enterprises Development in Srilanka (ed) "*Women in Micro and and Small Enterprise Development*" Dignard. L and Hvet. J Boulder: Westview Press.

Sanjay Diwari and Anusha Diwari (2007)" "*Women Entrepreneurship and Economic Development*", Sarup & Sons Publishers, New Delhi.

Schumpeter. J.A. (1934) "*The Theory of Economic Development*" Cambridge Mass; Harverd University Press.

Singh B.K. (2006) "*Women Empowerment Through Self-Help Groups*", Adhyayan Publishers, Delhi.

Weber, M. (1930) "The *Protestant Ethic and the Sprit of Capitalism*", Translated by Parsons", Scribner, New York.

JOURNALS

Adereni M.O, Liori H.O, Siyanbola W.O, Adegbite and Adebereijo S.A (2008) "An Assessment of the Choice and Performance of Women Entrepreneurs in Technological and Non Technological Enterprises in South Western Nigeria," *African Journal of Business Management*, Vol. 2, No. 10, October, pp. 165-176.

Ajit Kanitkar (1994) "Entrepreneurs and Micro-Enterprises in Rural India "*Economic and Political Weakly*, Vol. xxix , No. 1, February.

Alexandar L.Anna, Gayler N.Chandler, Erik Jansen, P.Mero (2000)" Women Business Owners in Traditional & Non-traditional Industries", *Journal of Business Venturing*, Vol. 15, No. 3 May, pp. 279-303.

Alicia. M. Robb (2002) "Entrepreneurial Performance by Women and Minorities: The Case of New Firms", *Journal of Development Entrepreneurship*, Vol. 7, No. 4, December.

Almas Heshmati (2001) "On the Growth of Micro and Small Firms; Evidence from Sweden", *Small Business Economics*, Vol. 17, pp. 213-228.

Anna de Bruin (1999) "Women *and Entrepreneurship- Rationale for Micro Enterprise Development*", Paper Presented at the APEC Study Centre Consortium Conference, Auckland, May 31-June 2.

Arne L. Kalleberg and Kevin.T Leicht (1991) "Gender and Organisational Performance: Determinants of Small Business Survival and Success", *Academy of Management Journal*, Vol. 34, No. 1, pp. 136-161.

Barth. F (1967) "On the Study of Social Change" *American Anthropologist*, Vol. 68, December, pp. 661-669.

Barbara Entwisle, Gail E. Hendrson, Susan E.Short, Jill Bouma, Zhai Fengying (1995) "Gender and Family Business in Rural China", *American Sociological Review*, Vol. 60, February pp. 36-57.

Bhagyavathi, Venugopal, Nagesha G & Nagabhusanam K (2008) " Participation Level of Farm Women in Entrepreneurship Activities Under Self-Help Groups", *Mysore Journal of Agricultural Science*, Vol. 42, No. 1, pp. 159-162.

Botha. M, Nieman G.H and Van Vuumen (2006) "Evaluating the Women Entrepreneurship Training Programme: A South African Study" *The International Indigenous Journal of Entrepreneurship*, Vol. 2, No. 1, October.

Carl Liedholm (2002) "Small Firm Dynamics: Evidence from Africa and Latin America", *Small Business Economics*, Vol. 18, No. 1/3, Special Issue: Small Firm Dynamism in East Asia, pp. 227-242.

Carole E.Scoot (1986)" Why More Women are Becoming Entrepreneurs", *Journal of Small Business Management*, Vol. 24. No. 4, October pp. 37-50.

Chitsike Colletah (2000) "Cultural as a Barrier to Rural Women's Entrepreneurship; Experience from Zimbabwe", *Gender and Development*, Vol. 8, No. 1, pp. 71-77.

Collerette. P and Aubry P. (1990) "Socio-Economic Evolution of Women Business Owners in Quebec -1989", *Journal of Business Ethics*, Vol. 9, pp. 417, 422.

Elizabeth Walker and Bererly Webster (2006) "Management Competencies of Women Business Owners," *Entrepreneurship Management*, Vol. 2, pp. 495-508.

Eshetu Bekele and Zelete Worku (2008) "Women Entrepreneurship in Micro Small and Medium Enterprises: The Case of Ethiopia", *Journal of International Women Studies*, Vol. 10 No. 2, November, pp. 3-18.

Evans David.S. Jovanovic Boyan (1989) An Estimate Model of Entrepreneurial Choice Under Liquidity Constraints", *Journal of Political Economy*, Vol. 97, No. 4, pp. 8008.

Femida Handy, Bhagyashree Renade, Meena Kasam (2007) "To Profit to Non-Profit Women Entrepreneurs in India", *Non Profit Management and Leadership*. Vol. 17, No. 7, pp. 383-399.

Francis M.Hill, Claire M.Leitch & Richard M.Harrison (2006) "Desperately Seeking Finance? The Demand for Finance by Women Owned and Led business", *Venture Capital*, Vol. 8, No. 2, April. pp. 159-182.

Gray R.Kenneth and Joycelyn Finley Harvey (2005) "Women and Entrepreneurship in Morocco-Debunking Stereo Types and Discerning Strategies" *International Entrepreneurship and Management Journal*, Vol. 1, pp. 203-217.

Greg Hundly (2000) "Male/Female Earning Differences in Self-employment: The Effects of Marriage, Children and the Household Division of Labour", *Industrial and Labour Relation Review,* Vol. 54, No. 1, October.

Gundry L.K.(2001) "The Ambitious Entrepreneurs: High Growth Strategies of Women Owned Enterprises", *Journal of Business Venturing*, Vol. 16, No. 4, September, pp. 453-470.

Hatun Ufuk and "ozen "ozan (2001) " The Profile of Women Entrepreneurs". *International Journal of Consumer Studies"*, Vol. 25, No. 4, December. pp. 299-308.

Heikki Haino (2006) "Use of Borrowed Start –up Capital and Micro Enterprise in Mexico. Existence of Liquidity Constraints", *Portuguese Economic Journal.*, Vol. 5, No. 1, pp. 1-30.

Helen Ruth Appas (2004) "Minority Women's Micro Enterprises in Rural Areas of the United States of America, Africa American, Hespanic American and Native American Case Studies", *Geo Journal*, Vol. 61, pp. 281-289.

Holy Buttner. E. "(2001) "Examining Female Entrepreneur's Management Style: An Application of a Relational Frame", *Journal of Business Ethics*, Vol. 29, pp. 253-269.

Ingoid Verheul and Roy Thorik (2001) "Start-up Capital "Does Gender Matter", *Small Business Economics*, Vol. 16, pp. 329-35.

Ingoid Verheul, Martin Carree and Roy Thorik (2009) "Allocation and Productivity of Time in New Ventures of Female and Male Entrepreneurs" *Small Business Economics*, Vol. 33, No.3, pp. 273-291.

Joan Winn (2005) "Women Entrepreneurs; Can We Remove the Barriers." *International Entrepreneurship and Management Journal*, Vol. 1, pp. 381-397.

Karyn. A.Loscocco and Kevin T.Leich (1993) "Gender Work-family Linkages and Economic Success Among Small Business Owners" *Journal of Marriage and Family*, Vol. 55, November, pp. 875-887.

Karyn. A. Loscocco and Joyce Robinson (1991) "Barriers to Women's Small Business Success in the United States" *Gender & Society*, Vol. 5, No. 4, December, pp. 511-532.

Kathleen Dechant and Asya & L.Lanky (2005) "Toward an Understanding of Arab Women Entrepreneurs in Bahrain and Oman", *Journal of Development Entrepreneurship*, Vol. 10, No. 2, pp. 123-140.

Lee M.A & Michel S. Rendell (2001) "Self-Employment Disadvantage in the Working Lives of Blacks and Females", *Population Research and Policy Review*, Vol. 20, pp. 291-320.

Loscocco K.A, Robinson A.J, Richard H. Hell and John. K. Allen (1991) "Gender and Small Business Success," *Social Force*, Vol. 70, No. 1, September, pp. 65-85.

Luis M.Shellon (2006) "Female Entrepreneurs, Work-Family Conflict and Venture Performance: New Insights into the Work-Family Interface," *Journal of Small Business Management*, Vol. 44, No. 2, pp. 285-297.

Mahmud Rahman khan (1995) "Women Entrepreneurs in the Bangladeshi Restaurant Business", *Development Practice*, Vol. 5, No. 3, August, pp. 240-246.

Morris Michel H, Nola N. Miyasaki, Craig E.Watters, and Susam. M Coombes (2006) "The Dilemma of Growth: Understanding Venture Size Choices of Women Entrepreneurs", *Journal of Small Business Management*, Vol. 144, No. 2 pp. 221-241.

Muriel Orhan (2001) "Women Business Owners in France – The Issues of Financing Discrimination", *Journal of Small Business Management*, Vol. 39, No. 1, pp. 95-102.

Miri Lerner, Candida Brush & Rober Hirrich (1997) "Israeli Women Entrepreneurs: An Examination of Factors Affecting Performance", *Journal of Business Venturing*, Vol. 12, November-July, pp. 315-339.

Monica Belcourt (1990) "A Family Portrait of Canada's Most Successful Female Entrepreneurs", *Journal of Business Ethics*, Vol. 9, pp. 435-438.

Muhammad Azam Roomi and Guy Parrot (2008) "Barriers to Development and Progression of Women Entrepreneurs in Pakistan" *The Journal of Entrepreneurship*, Vol. 17, No. 1, pp. 59-72.

Neider. L (1987) "A Preliminary Investigation of Female Entrepreneur in Florida", *Journal of Small Business Management*, Vol. 25, No. 3. pp. 22-29.

Nelson G.W (1989) "Factors of Friendship: Relevance of Significant Others to Female Business Owners", *Entrepreneurship Theory & Practice*, Vol. 13, No. 4, pp. 7-18.

Pillai N.C & Anna V. (1990) "The Entrepreneurial Spirit Among Women — A Study in Kerala", *Indian Management*. November-December, pp. 93-98.

Pooja Nayyar, Avinash Sharma, Jatinder Kishtwaria, Aruna Rana & Neena Vyas (2007)" Causes and Constraints Faced by Women Entrepreneurs in Entrepreneurial Process", *Journal of Social Science*, Vol. 14, No. 2, pp. 99-102.

Poonam Parihar, Sing D.K, Sharma V.K. and Sing R.P. (2008). Impact of Motivational Factors and Role Stress on Women Entrepreneurs in Jammu", *Indian Research Journal of Extension Education*," Vol. 8, No. 2 & 3, pp. 73.76.

Priscilla Chu (2000) "The Characteristics of Chinese Female Entrepreneurs: Motivation and Personality", *Journal of Enterprising Culture*, Vol. 8, No. 1, March, pp. 67-84.

Rao.C HariNarayana (1991) "Promotion of Women Entrepreneurship, SEDME Journal, Vol. 18, No. 3, pp. 21-28.

Ranjaini N (2008) "Management Training Needs Women Entrepreneurs" *Anthropologist*, Vol. 10, No. 4, pp. 277-281.

Robert. D. Hisrich & Candida Brush (1984)" The Women Entrepreneur Management Skills and Business Problem" *Journal of Small Business Management*, Vol. 22, No. 1, pp. 30-37.

Rebort D. Hisrich & Gyula Fulop (1994) "The Role of Women Entrepreneurs in Hungary's Transition Economy" *International Studies of Management & Organisation*, Vol. 24, No. 4, pp. 100-117.

Sherri Grasmuck and Rosario Espinal (2000), "Market Success or Female Autonomy? Income, Ideology, and Empowerment Among Micro Entrepreneurs in the Dominican Republic", *Gender and Society*, Vol. 14, No. 2, pp. 231-255.

Selvamalar Ayadurai M. Sadia Sohaul (2006) "Profile of Women Entrepreneurs in a War-torn Area. A Case Study of North East Sri Lanka", *Journal of Development Entrepreneurship*, Vol. 11, No. 1, pp. 3-17.

Shiva Malik & Taranjit Kaur Rao (2008) "Profile of Women Entrepreneurs—A Case Study of Chandigarh" Political Economy Journal of India, Vol. No. January-June.

Shivani Sharma & Gurprit Singh Dhillon (2008) "Identification of Prospects and Problems of Women Entrepreneurs of Punjab Through SWOT" *Indian Journal of Social Research*, Vol. 49 , No. 3, July-September, pp. 245-257.

Skinner D. Sandra (1992) Female Entrepreneurs in the Retail Trade: A Study of Personal and Professional Traits as they Impact on Business Environments", *The International Review of Retail Distribution and Consumer Research*, Vol. 2, No. 2, pp. 183-195.

Stanley Cromie (1987) "Motivations of Aspiring Male and Female Entrepreneurs", *Journal of Occupational Behaviour*, Vol. 8, pp. 251-261.

Spinder Dhaliwal (2000) "Asian Female Entrepreneurs and Women in Business –An Exploratory Study " *Entrepreneurs and Women Management Studies* , Vol. 1, No. 2, pp. 207-216.

Tracy Bachrach Ehlers and Karen Mein (1998) "Women and the False Promise of Micro Enterprise", *Gender and Society*, Vol. 12, No. 4, pp. 424-440.

Williams. D.A (2008) "Export Stimulation in Micro and Small Locally Owned Firms from Emerging Environments: New Evidence", *Journal of International Entrepreneurship*, Vol. 6, pp. 101-102.

Xavier M.J , Raja J, Usha Nandhini.S, (2008), Impact Assessment of a Rural Women's Micro Entrepreneurship Project Using Path Analysis Models" *IIMB Management Review*, Vol. 20, No. 2, June.

Zapalska, A (1997) "A Profile of Women Entrepreneurs and Enterprises in Poland," *Journal of Small Business Management*' Vol. 35, pp. 76-82.

REPORTS/WORKING PAPERS

Anna de Bruin (1999) "Women and Entrepreneurship-Rationale for Micro Enterprise Development", Paper Presented at the APEC study Centre Consortium Conference, Auckland, May 31-June 2.

Government of India, Census India Report 2001, Office of the Register General and Census Commissioner, New Delhi.

Government of Tamil Nadu, (2010), Official Records Maintained by Project Implementation Unit, Mahalir Thittam, District Collector Office, Coimbatore, 2010.

Government of Tamil Nadu, (2010), Scheme on Mahalir Thittam by the Tamil Nadu Corporation for Development of Women Ltd., Ministry of Rural Development, Chennai.

International Labour Organisation (1998), Gender Issues in Micro-Enterprise Development: A Briefing Note, The International Small Enterprise Programme (ISEP), June.

Jaria M, Laily . P Mumtazha .O, & Aini .S, (2003) " Report on Mechanisation & Technological Adoption: Scaling up Micro Enterprises to Small scale enterprise: Serdang: Monograph Series on Social Science, Penerbit University, Putra Malaysia.

WEBSITES

Rao M.B (2007) "A Small Business - An Avenue of Self Employment" online Paper available at www.indianmba.com/Faculty_Column/FC527/fc527.html.

Census of India available at www.censusindia.gov.in

Index